D0933841

Döpfner, Mathias,
The trade trap : dealing with
democracies and dictators /
2023.
33305256836622
ca   09/26/23

THE TRADE TRAP

HOW TO STOP DOING BUSINESS WITH DICTATORS

MATHIAS DÖPFNER

SIMON & SCHUSTER

New York   London   Toronto   Sydney   New Delhi

Simon & Schuster
1230 Avenue of the Americas
New York, NY 10020

Copyright © 2023 by Mathias Döpfner

All rights reserved, including the right to reproduce this book or portions thereof in any form whatsoever. For information, address Simon & Schuster Subsidiary Rights Department, 1230 Avenue of the Americas, New York, NY 10020.

First Simon & Schuster hardcover edition September 2023

SIMON & SCHUSTER and colophon are registered trademarks of Simon & Schuster, Inc.

For information about special discounts for bulk purchases, please contact Simon & Schuster Special Sales at 1-866-506-1949 or business@simonandschuster.com.

The Simon & Schuster Speakers Bureau can bring authors to your live event. For more information or to book an event, contact the Simon & Schuster Speakers Bureau at 1-866-248-3049 or visit our website at www.simonspeakers.com.

Interior design by Wendy Blum

Manufactured in the United States of America

10 9 8 7 6 5 4 3 2 1

Library of Congress Cataloging-in-Publication Data

Names: Döpfner, Mathias, author.
Title: The trade trap : dealing with democracies and dictators / Mathias Döpfner.
Description: New York : Simon and Schuster, [2023] | Includes index.
Identifiers: LCCN 2023014005 (print) | LCCN 2023014006 (ebook) |
    ISBN 9781668016251 (hardcover) | ISBN 9781668016268 (paperback) |
    ISBN 9781668016275 (ebook)
Subjects: LCSH: Free trade—Political aspects. | International trade—Political
    aspects. | Democracy—Economic aspects. | Foreign economic relations.
Classification: LCC HF1713 .D67 2023 (print) | LCC HF1713 (ebook) |
    DDC 382/.71—dc23/eng/20230505
LC record available at https://lccn.loc.gov/2023014005
LC ebook record available at https://lccn.loc.gov/2023014006

ISBN 978-1-6680-1625-1
ISBN 978-1-6680-1627-5 (ebook)

To my children.

"The secret to happiness is freedom and the secret to freedom is courage."

most likely Pericles, circa 495–429 BC

CONTENTS

CONTENTS

IV. THE ANSWER: FREEDOM TRADE

THE
TRADE
TRAP

PREFACE
MY LOVE FOR DEMOCRACY

I love democracy. Democracy is freedom. Democracy is humor. Democracy is respect. Democracy is compromise. Democracy is frivolity. Democracy is competition and creativity. Democracy is contradictory. Democracy makes mistakes—just like us humans.

I love democracy because it is the opposite of Auschwitz, the Holocaust's largest extermination camp. Auschwitz is a global symbol of inhumanity. It stands for genocide and hatred and arbitrary power—everything that is possible where democracy is absent.

When democracy is vigorous and intact, it protects us from genocide, hatred, and arbitrary power.

And I'm afraid of arbitrary power. I remember a night on a work trip to Moscow, back in 1988—Soviet times. I was visiting a Russian pianist I represented for the artists management agency I worked for. That night, I was driven alone in a taxi through icy, snowy, dark streets, to a restaurant someone had recommended. Down in the cellar you could get Crimean champagne and caviar. It didn't taste good to me, because I couldn't shake the feeling that someone might come and take me away. Why would they? I hadn't done anything wrong. I wasn't being threatened. There was no particular reason for my concern. But I knew of the kind of arbitrary power that existed in the Soviet Union. I had been warned by the pianist that my hotel room was most likely bugged and that I should put on some music while speaking. Experiencing such fear was profound after a life in a free country. I never wanted to feel that way again. It taught me to love democracy.

Democracies are far from perfect. They make lots of mistakes, including ones that resemble or are even identical to those made by autocracies. But there's a big difference: In democracies you get to criticize the mistakes. There are almost always people who do. And if there are enough of them, then there are consequences.

Equally, democracy is the promise that I can be accused of something and still be given a fair chance—in a court of law with my very own lawyer and an independent judge. Put simply, it's about the dignity of the individual—the citizen—rather than the arbitrary actions of authority. The rule of law is the oxygen of democracy. It would suffocate without it. That's why things such as the Berlin District Court exist. Or the Idaho Supreme Court. In courts big and small throughout the democratic world, prosecutors, defense lawyers, and impartial judges try to make fair and just decisions. They protect those who are weaker from those who are stronger, and ensure that everyone has the same rights before the law. I used to think the rule of law was a technicality, less important than freedom and democracy. Today, I am convinced it is their foundation. The law is civilization's most important achievement, far superior to the "law" of the jungle. In Darwinian nature, the fittest—those who run faster or are physically more powerful—win. But in civilizations based on the rule of law, those who are weaker stand a chance too. There's justice.

That is democracy's core promise.

That is why I love democracy.

That is why we must protect democracy.

That is why we need a values-based trade alliance of democracies.

And that is why I wrote this book.

The idea for this book came about shortly after Russia's annexation of Crimea in 2014. It was a time when the CEOs of most global companies were raving about opportunities in the Chinese market. Anyone who questioned the reliability of these kinds of business links was labeled a killjoy.

I began to think about a values-based trade policy in 2015. I was convinced we needed a better solution than just a unilateral decoupling. And I came up with the idea of a new democratic and transatlantic trade alliance that would strengthen democracies to grow independent of dictators. The people I ran it past were critical: The vision was unrealistic, unaffordable, naïve, and dangerous. Good friends warned me that my reputation would suffer. All who benefit from doing business with nondemocratic countries would try to discredit this book. It would be best to drop it, they said, and so I did.

A few years later, I wrote a synopsis for the book anyway, and sent it both to the literary agent Andrew Wylie and a big German publisher. The response of the publisher was less than enthusiastic: It was an absurd idea. What made me think I was qualified to write on this topic? I'd be better off just giving speeches instead.

And then, when the Ukraine war began in February 2022 and pretty much everything turned out as I'd predicted—Andrew Wylie called me up and said I should try again: "Mathias, you have to write this book."

This book isn't about economics, even though it contains quite a few figures. It is a book about the future. While it includes extensive discussion of politics, it's mostly about us, the citizens of democracies. Our behavior. Our values. And the consequences of our actions. It's about the future of our freedom.

The book combines my experience as the CEO of an international media company—my role has helped my convictions develop and mature—with objective analysis and sober facts. I'm also adding in some robust personal opinions and commentary.

The book has no party political agenda. It is about strengthening democracy. Does that mean fostering the renaissance of "neocon" politics or rather "liberal" dreams? No. It's a bipartisan necessity. It is as impartial and ideologically unpredictable as I am. For the Left, I am too far to the Right. And for the Right, I am too far to the Left. I don't fit into any political box, which is appropriate for a publisher, I think.

The idea I outline in this book may seem impossible at first glance. And yes, it is hardly achievable immediately. But there is a wonderful saying, attributed to Otto von Bismarck: "Politics is the art of the possible." That saying is often misunderstood—especially by politicians—to mean that politics can only do what is possible in a given moment. This is more or less the opposite of what Bismarck meant, because otherwise politics wouldn't be an art. Anyone could do it and there would be no need for politicians. The "art of the possible" actually has more to do with making possible, at any given moment, what seems impossible. That is the art—and also the craft—of politics.

Viewed like this, much more is possible than we think. Sometimes even the impossible.

Thirty Minutes with
Vladimir Putin

I was invited to a conversation in the Kremlin in 2005, a few months after Paul Klebnikov, the editor of Forbes Russia, *was killed right outside the magazine's Moscow offices. At the time,* Forbes Russia *was a licensed edition of the American magazine published in Russia by the Axel Springer publishing group, of which I had been CEO for two years.*

On July 9, 2004, leaving work late at night, Paul was attacked by unidentified gunmen, who shot him nine times from a slow-moving car. A father of three young children, he initially survived the attack, but died in the hospital when the elevator taking him to the operating theater got stuck between two floors. Witnesses described the attack as an assassination. Commentators speculated that a Forbes Russia *story about the tax affairs of Russia's one hundred richest individuals might have prompted the ambush. Some reckoned oligarchs were behind the murder; others, the government itself.*

Our meeting was organized by the German government. The

aim: to encourage our publishing company to keep doing business in Russia.

In the early morning hours of January 20, 2005, I flew to Moscow from Berlin and spent almost three hours inching through the traffic jam on the monumental road that leads to the city center and Red Square. As soon as I arrived at the Kremlin, my cell phone was confiscated (weeks later, I could still hear Russian voices during calls and on my voicemail; I ultimately changed my handset and number). I was escorted through labyrinthine corridors to a reception room where an interpreter was waiting for me. There was some coffee and sparkling water. When the appointed time rolled round, nothing happened. Half an hour later, still nothing, and no indication of how long the delay would be.

After an hour or so, I got the interpreter to ask the secretary what was going on. Her response: All of this is normal, the president has important matters to attend to, it isn't possible to give an exact time, please have another coffee. I thought of the legendary trip my company's founder, Axel Springer, made to Moscow in 1958. He had to wait for two weeks before Nikita Khrushchev finally received him. Was Putin trying to copy this? Two and a half hours later—and after another five or so inquiries on my part—I wasn't just annoyed by the blatant humiliation ritual, but also genuinely concerned. There was a crucial board meeting in Berlin the following morning which I couldn't afford to miss. Given the airport's operating hours and the three-hour drive back, I was going to be compelled to say something in order to get home in time. Politely, I explained my dilemma to the wide-eyed secretary, and said that unfortunately, I'd have to postpone the meeting if it didn't take place within the next hour. They clearly weren't expecting this. Lots of commotion ensued: Men started scurrying around the office, doors slammed. Then, after half an hour, the big moment arrived. The president was ready.

Together with the interpreter and a Kremlin aide, I stood before an oversized double door. It suddenly opened onto a never-ending ceremonial hall with ornate, gold-leaf stucco ceilings. A guard gestured to me that I should wait. Only when Vladimir Putin entered through the opposite door was I allowed to start walking. Protocol dictated we meet in the exact center of the room—every movement precisely orchestrated like a court ritual. We took our prescribed seats at a gigantic table. The interpreter sat beside us but never uttered a single word. Putin spoke in a low voice that was difficult to understand, but in excellent, almost accent-free German with a slight Saxonian lilt.

He opened the discussion by saying how much he regretted the Klebnikov incident and that our publishing company must not, under any circumstances, let this terrible event deter it from doing business in Russia. The crime would be investigated as a matter of utmost urgency. We will find the perpetrators, he said in what was practically a whisper, forcing me to lean forward to catch his words. We will find them, he promised. You can be sure of that.

Then we moved on to broader issues. One part of the conversation lodged itself in my memory. Putin said that Chechen terrorism was a major challenge for his country. I asked: Isn't the fight against Islamism arguably a common challenge, and thus a common concern for the United States, the EU, and Russia? Yes, he replied, we have many commonalities and shared concerns. And then he uttered the crucial words: If only the United States would stop treating us like a colony. Our Russian culture is much older *than theirs, our feelings run much deeper than theirs. We have our own traditions, we have our own sense of pride. We are not an American colony.*

And there it was, flashing away quite unmistakably: the wounded pride of the head of a former superpower, which now found itself downgraded to middling status. He was consumed with an ambition to change precisely this status, an ambition that would take an increasingly radicalized form over the next few years. Even then, in that earlier phase, which looks relatively benign from today's perspective, it still felt unsettling, and dangerous.

After a few more turns on the conversational merry-go-round, and exactly thirty minutes later, Putin brought the discussion to a close. I hear you're in a hurry, he said. Don't worry, we'll give you an escort to the airport to speed things up.

With motorcycles riding in formation both in front of and behind my car, blue lights flashing, and megaphones blaring, we raced to the airport. It was a demonstration of power, intimidating for all concerned. I sat behind my car window, hiding from outside viewers and feeling embarrassed. I reached the airport much too early.

Following the murder of our editor, we kept the magazine open and didn't change a thing editorially. Its coverage remained just as critical as before. We held our course when, years later, the mayor of Moscow threatened another editor in a bid to stop the publication of an article about his wife. And especially during the annexation of Crimea in 2014, when our publication took a highly independent stance that criticized the government.

The conflict was finally resolved in a different way. In 2014, the Russian government passed a law limiting the foreign holdings of Russian media to 20 percent—a law that took effect in 2017 with retroactive force. As a result, we would have to sell 80 percent of our business to a Russian national. We were discreetly informed of the expectation to find a pro-government buyer. That way, we could continue making money in Russia, but editorial control would be in "safer" hands. The Axel Springer publishing group instead "sold" 100 percent of the business for a symbolic price to a regime critic.

The damage to the company was considerable and the conclusion obvious: It would have been better if we had never done business in Russia.

PART I

THE STATUS QUO: OLD AND NEW ENEMIES

DEMOCRACY ON THE DEFENSIVE

Some ideas write history. Some ideas describe history. But some ideas shape history.

Writing history: In 1992, political scientist Francis Fukuyama published his famous book *The End of History and the Last Man*. As early as 1989—influenced by the fall of the Berlin Wall—he'd already outlined his core idea in an article for a small foreign policy journal, *The National Interest*: "What we may be witnessing is not just the end of the Cold War, or the passing of a particular period of postwar history, but the end of history as such: that is, the end point of mankind's ideological evolution and the universalization of Western liberal democracy as the final form of human government." "The triumph of the West, of the Western idea," he wrote, "is evident first of all in the total exhaustion of viable systematic alternatives to Western liberalism."

Describing history: In 2015, historian Yuval Noah Harari's book *Homo Deus* predicted a new, godlike era for humanity, because all of its old problems and limitations had been overcome:

"At the dawn of the third millennium, humanity wakes up to an amazing realization. Most people rarely think about it, but in the last few decades we have managed to rein in famine, plague and war. Of course, these problems have not been completely solved, but they have been transformed from incomprehensible and uncontrollable forces of nature into manageable challenges. We don't need to pray to any god or saint to rescue us from them. We know quite well what needs to be done in order to prevent famine, plague and war—and we usually succeed in doing it."

Shaping history: This is what the world-famous maxim "*Wandel durch Handel*" tried to do. It originated in the 1960s, when Berlin politician Egon Bahr dubbed *Ostpolitik*, the West German outreach to the nations of the Eastern Bloc, "change through rapprochement." This then morphed into "*Wandel durch Handel*," or "change through trade"—a hope, promise, and incantation that appeared without fail in speeches by Chancellors Helmut Kohl and Gerhard Schröder in the 1980s and 1990s when calling for an intensification of economic relations with China or Russia. Bankers also liked to use the concept when courting undemocratic countries.

These three famous quotes have one thing in common: They were considered visionary and realistic. Today, in the third decade of the third millennium, they have turned out to be wrong and even dangerous. In essence, they were too optimistic in their assumptions: Democracy had triumphed. Famines, epidemics, and wars had been overcome. And as long as we did as much business as possible with undemocratic states and dictatorships, things would take a liberal turn there too. Three false promises. Three utopias shattered by reality.

Democracy and freedom have not prevailed across the

globe. On the contrary: They are globally in retreat. Free and open societies are facing a number of existential threats. For the seventeenth year in a row, independent think tank Freedom House has recorded a decline in democracy, and now speaks of a "long freedom recession." It has downgraded more and more countries from "Free" to "Partly Free" and then from "Partly Free" to "Not Free." Only 20 percent of the world's population live in countries that are "Free." And 40 percent live in states that are "Not Free." This is the highest level since 1997. Viewed objectively, freedom is on the defensive all around the world.

According to projections by Bloomberg Economics, the share of global production by "free" or "mostly free" economies is projected to decline from around 60 percent in 2000 to 33 percent in 2050. The share of those classified as "mostly unfree"—that is, economies with high levels of state ownership and control—is projected to rise from 12 percent to 43 percent. So the story is far from over. In fact, it's only just beginning to get really dangerous again.

Hunger, disease, and war are not under control. They have not vanished. They're back with a vengeance and now dominate our lives. War is raging in Ukraine, and even the most advanced science hasn't managed to halt the COVID-19 pandemic. And because a dictator has chosen to block grain and gas deliveries, people in Africa and beyond are starving.

Nor has "*Wandel durch Handel*" succeeded in shaping history as so many hoped. In fact, the maxim of "change through trade" has led to a macabre outcome that's quite the opposite of the one intended: Instead of becoming more liberal, tolerant, and cosmopolitan through intensified business links with Western democracies, the world's autocracies, like Russia and China, have become even more radical and undemocratic. So there has been "change through trade," but this change ended up weakening democracy rather than strengthening it and effectively led the West into a trade trap.

The world order looks fragile. Politically and economically, the West is weaker than it has been in decades. And unless we make fundamental changes, this will be the beginning of the end of democracy. Lack of freedom will vanquish freedom.

The multilateral institutions created after World War II are weak or dysfunctional or corrupt, or all three. Most obviously, the U.N. has transformed into the opposite of its founding idea: Instead of securing world peace and ensuring respect for international law and human rights, it has turned into a bureaucratic monster, where rogue states forge majority alliances that make a mockery of democracies and spare dictatorships from unpleasant interventions. Judicial appointments in Iceland are framed as a scandalous human rights violation, so that no one has to talk about the Uyghur camps in China.

The World Health Organization (WHO) has evolved from an organization with medical aims to an institution shaped by political factors, which became completely clear during the pandemic. An independent panel of experts appointed by WHO has since concluded that it did not act quickly enough and should have declared a state of emergency well before January 30, 2020. Chinese ophthalmologist Li Wenliang had already warned about the virus at the start of January, before being interrogated by the police and silenced. When the outbreak could no longer be hushed up, the Communist leadership resorted to drastic measures that were incompatible with a respect for human rights. And yet, for a long time the Chinese government's crisis management was praised by

WHO. This blind faith in China gave the world a pandemic that has so far led to around 7 million deaths.

Seventy years after its founding, the European Union is also in the throes of a deep identity crisis. At least since the 2015 refugee crisis, the EU bureaucracies in Brussels and Strasbourg have seemed less a part of the solution and more a symbol of the problem itself. Even the simplest logistical challenge—the orderly distribution of refugees—led to chaos and discord. Britain drew its own conclusions in the Brexit referendum of 2016, when the country left the European club. A few years later, when it came to ordering COVID-19 vaccines, the EU blocked its member states from acting independently, only to waste precious months procuring the vaccines itself. The UK and the United States struck their first deals with AstraZeneca in May 2020, while the EU took around three months longer. And this despite the fact that Astra-Zeneca is a European company. EU officials allegedly spent two months on legislation relating to vaccine order contracts. The EU dragged not only its feet when obtaining vaccines, but when distributing them as well. On average, the EU took sixty-three days to administer the first dose to 5 percent of its population. That was more than three weeks longer than the United States and the UK.

The World Trade Organization (WTO) is another particularly sorry case of good intentions gone wrong. The date that marks its key strategic failure is December 11, 2001, when China was admitted as a full member after fifteen years of negotiations. A great day for China, but possibly the biggest mistake Western market economies have made in recent history. Compiling GDP data from the World Bank into a simple model illustrates the absurdity of the problem in a nutshell: Since China's accession to the WTO, the United States' share of global GDP has fallen from

31.47 percent in 2001 to 24.15 percent in 2021. Europe's share fell from 21.99 percent to 17.79 percent. China, on the other hand, has grown its share from 3.98 percent to over 18.32 percent in the same period: An almost fivefold increase in just two decades. China's share of global CO_2 emissions skyrocketed in a similar way—growing threefold since joining the WTO. In 2021, China was responsible for 32.87 percent of the world's carbon emissions. That's more than the subsequent five largest polluting countries combined. Any climate policy without China would thus be pointless.

The fundamental error was to expose market economies to a state-led capitalism that creates its own rules, and abuses existing terms of trade and competition. Asymmetry instead of reciprocity, fueled by China's ongoing status as a developing country—a status that allows China to benefit from looser rules within the WTO. A status that is absurd for an economic superpower like China. The process of "change through trade" was actually implemented back to front: As the West became weaker, China grew in economic strength and authority. The Centre for Economics and Business Research (CEBR) predicts that China will overtake America as the world's largest economy by 2036. If we keep heading down this road, China will continue to gain in economic power and dominance, which will lead to increased political influence. The end point is heavy economic and political dependence on China, resulting in a stepwise system change. That can have only one outcome: the decline of democratic economies and societies.

Until recently, such scenarios were dismissed as scaremongering, but Putin's aggression toward Ukraine has changed everything. Russia's invasion and its fatal consequences for Europe and the wider world have been the most brutal wake-up call imaginable. A *Zeitenwende* or "watershed moment," as German chancellor Olaf Scholz put it. A moment of huge disillusionment. And proof that appeasement, whether related to security or economic policies, works no better in the twenty-first century than it did in the twentieth. After the annexation of Crimea, only a military alliance and hard-line stance could have stopped further encroachment from Putin—not lucrative gas contracts or projects such as Nord Stream 2. But war seemed unimaginable to most. A cyberwar perhaps, or an arms race involving AI and data, but surely not a conventional war in the heart of Europe with soldiers, tanks, and aerial raids in order to gain territory and topple governments—that seemed unthinkable.

The aggressiveness of an autocratic and totalitarian leader like Putin surprised many democratic politicians. They didn't think that he would follow through, because they projected their own psychology and mechanisms onto the leader of an autocratic system. This is a mistake the West has made time and again when dealing with nondemocratic systems and their despots: Iran, Iraq, Syria, Saudi Arabia, and, of course, China. Now that the unthinkable has happened, even the impossible seems possible. It has suddenly become clear that China could deal with Taiwan the way Putin dealt with Crimea. And that this, as in Russia's case, might only be a first step rather than the last. Even the most optimistic observer has realized that China might pursue its global geostrategic ambitions not just with data and dollars, but with weapons and warriors. The Russian war is a mere proxy for the real conflict between the U.S. and China. Putin's attack is a final warning and the catalyst for a major conceptual rethink.

"Change through rapprochement" ended up being "change through opportunism." In this kind of scenario, a set of values-based foreign, security, and trade policies is not idealistic. It is pragmatic. It is a strategic necessity for the continued existence of democracy.

Whether it's Joe Biden or Olaf Scholz, Western heads of state have left no room for doubt in their recent speeches and actions: What we are witnessing is a battle between democracies and autocracies. Today, our world order feels dystopian. Freedom and democracy are threatened by war, dictators, autocrats, populists, and weak leadership within open societies, and also by well-meaning but growing restrictions on freedom in the fight against climate change and the pandemic.

What is uniquely dangerous about the current situation is the sheer accumulation of threats. A modern society can cope with a war, a recession, inflation, a pandemic, and even long-term challenges such as climate change. But things become much trickier when they combine.

The dominant feeling in the world's strongest democracies is overload, disorder, alienation, and threat. The consequences are polarization, division, and exclusion. We are witnessing rejection on a grand scale: First one group rejects another, then individuals cancel each other on a very personal basis. The importance of the collective diminishes. The individual is at the forefront of an ever more narcissistic Instagram society.

Major political parties are losing support. There's an overall disenchantment with institutions. Unions, churches, NGOs, and corporations with household names have lost their charisma. Established media brands are disappearing, and those that remain have largely lost their authority. Many long-respected media outlets are trying to prevent the disintegration of democracy with all their might, but often act in such a one-sided way that they accelerate the process.

At the same time, society is getting used to the fact that the state will help cushion the financial consequences of major crises such as the pandemic or the war in Ukraine. Huge government assistance packages have considerably softened the impact of brutal market forces, and citizens are gradually growing accustomed to a new type of government-sponsored capitalism. Even if not yet comparable in terms of the form it takes, the Chinese model of state capitalism is quietly knocking on American and European doors.

The fact that the old rule no longer applies—namely that recessions go hand in hand with high unemployment—has a kind of tranquilizing effect. The huge scarcity of labor means that deep recessions are now perfectly possible with full employment. This new phenomenon obscures the seriousness of the situation. The decline of Western economies can be borne quite comfortably in a home office with a secure job and some subsidies from the state. Government-sponsored capitalism is like a sleeping pill for competitiveness.

All of this is troubling. Yet within this crisis—as in every crisis—lies a great opportunity. The open society is at a crossroads. Anything could happen. What we're experiencing could be the beginning of the end of free democracies. Or a wake-up call. The start of an era of strengthening and renewal.

The world order of the last seventy-five years is dissolving at high speed—driven by very weak leadership in most of the democracies and frighteningly strong leadership in many autocracies. A succession of European centuries and an American century have been followed if not yet by an Asian century by the beginning of an era of Chinese dominance. This, one might say, is the way of things. In the free play of market forces and competition, things will go up and down for all concerned. If, since the nineteenth century, hierarchical European society has proved to be weak and American meritocracy more successful, then so be it. And we should accept this outcome—even if China has pulled ahead of America for the foreseeable future—for there will always be winners and losers when market forces compete. One can, of course, make this kind of argument. But the problem is that the rules are skewed: This isn't a proper competition and the results are far from fair. Consequently, we shouldn't accept it.

This is fortunately the current consensus in an increasingly polarized America—across all fronts, on the Left and the Right, among Democrats and Republicans, entrepreneurs and politicians. It is perhaps the only truly bipartisan certainty: China's actions are dangerous. The emerging dependence on China is not in America's interest.

While the United States has decided to decouple from China, Europe is still hesitating and mulling things over. Ursula von der Leyen's derisking approach is trying to balance out economic interests and national security concerns. But this might not be enough. A new, more extensive model is needed to foster change. In the great game of market forces, old and new alliances are now being forged or deepened or destroyed. The United States can't decouple unilaterally without substantial long-term damage. American hubris—going solo under the banner of "America First"—would be a path to isolation and declining significance. But equally: There is no such thing as a European *Sonderweg*, individual sovereignty, or special path. Whether or not the United

States likes Europe's complexities and affectations, the two continents are fated to be interdependent, given that they jointly constitute the political powerhouse of a democratic and free social order. There is no room for the sovereignty or isolation of individual nations or of aggregate nations. There is only room for the sovereignty of democracy.

American preconceptions and judgments about Europe are well known and partly justified. But we shouldn't give up on Europe too soon. The growing polarization of our global power structures—on the one hand an America increasingly stifled by infighting and the constraints of political correctness, and on the other a China expanding its global dominance through state capitalism and data surveillance—actually offers Europe a historic opportunity. The continent of diversity, competitive ideas, intellectual property, sustainability, but above all a free and socially attractive lifestyle, could become a place of hope for young and ambitious people—"the European way of life" as a beacon for modernization. Is it likely? Or rather unlikely? I believe that the twenty-first century could still surprise us by becoming a new American-European era.

But we must decide between two possible paths.

Path 1: Putin and Xi continue their attempts to drive America and Europe apart. Europe, like Africa, grows increasingly dependent on China, evolving into a group of managed democracies with surveillance and severely limited freedom of expression. The "Old World" becomes a historically instructive theme park for tourists from all around the world. For example, they admire nature at its most pristine in the German state of Mecklenburg-Vorpommern, see historical traces of the Renaissance in Venice and Florence, and delight in Paris, the city of light and love. In this scenario, there is little value creation in Europe;

production largely takes place elsewhere. Russia and Islamist autocracies coordinate their interests and activities and become increasingly confident aggressors when enforcing their explicitly nondemocratic values. America isolates itself, and what was once the largest economy in the world becomes ever weaker politically and economically: yesterday's superpower. Representative democracy is slowly but steadily discarded by the wayward representatives of America's political extremes.

Path 2: A genuine transatlantic alliance is successfully revived as an economic- and values-based partnership and alternative to the U.S.'s unilateral decoupling from China. Offering freedom, security, dignity, and a sustainable way of life, founded on diversity and competition and achievement, it attracts the best of young global talent. The world's other democratic countries are drawn to join the alliance. This way, the free Western world secures a vital competitive advantage in the face of demographic shrinkage: long-term access to a well-educated workforce. In this scenario, China, with links to some Islamist states, becomes a strong but isolated power, weakened in the long run by its extreme homogeneity. Initially, post-Putin Russia will probably choose to rely on China, but perhaps in the end it will opt for the West after all. And one day, China too will realize that a little more freedom brings a great deal more prosperity.

In both of these scenarios, India is the crucial player in the overall power game. It might continue to work toward maximum neutrality under Narendra Modi or his successors—a kind of Switzerland with 1.4 billion inhabitants. Or it might join one of the key powers. A decisive factor here is whether an alliance with the United States and Europe looks attractive and inclusive enough. Should India, the most populous democracy on earth, opt to position itself on the wrong or the right side—however much one might still underestimate the country economically given its current levels of corruption and increased number of attacks on press freedom—it could have a pivotal effect.

Those seeking to foster the emergence of a reasonably stable world order, where a majority are committed to an open society, won't do so primarily through politics. And they most certainly won't do so through culture alone. The crucial incentive lies—as is almost always the case—in the economic sphere. And here, of course, discussion always turns first to China, although ultimately it's about more than just this one nation.

Russia's invasion of Ukraine has left the last remaining optimists painfully exposed. What truly matters, when push comes to shove, is values and rules. The late, but still timely lesson is: Anyone who doesn't share these values and rules can't be a reliable economic partner in the long term, let alone a strategic or security ally. Germany believed its energy dependence on Russia wasn't a problem because Russia would never cross the line and turn off the gas. But Russia did cross the line. It did the supposedly unthinkable. By the start of September 2022, it was clear that Europe would only get access to Russian gas if sanctions were lifted. China will act similarly in Taiwan, and one day cross the line. Just as Qatar or Saudi Arabia or other nondemocratic oil and energy caliphates will one day cross the line. And if they do, it will be because we let them. The West's big, recurring mistake is not believing that others might do what it is incapable of doing itself. Leaders of non-democracies frequently don't act in the best interests of their country or their people. They frequently don't act reasonably or ethically. They simply do what they want and whatever they can get away with.

Given all this, the problem has to be analyzed and solved more comprehensively, independent of current developments. It requires a new world trade order. It requires an economic alliance of democracies, with a clear set of conditions and a standing invitation to all nations to join it at any point.

One might question whether this problem should be solved at all. Or whether it's even possible to solve it—perhaps it's already much too late? There are countless arguments against the radically new notion of a values-based foreign and trade policy: It's unrealistic; the power of the status quo is simply too great; every big system change causes us too much damage. And so on.

But it is neither too late nor unrealistic. There are a few examples recognizing the urgency of the matter. Take Mario Draghi, a model for acting on principle and driving economic results. The experienced economist has turned Italy around in record time: from Europe's dysfunctional long tail to a model of reform and recovery. He successfully led Italy out of the pandemic and then freed it from the grip of Russia. No country has acted as consistently as Draghi's Italy following the outbreak of the war. Before that, Italy imported about 40 percent of its annual gas needs from Russia. Draghi was quick in closing deals with other states to reduce the energy dependence on Russia. As a result, Italy was better off than its European peers. Alone, such initiatives only have the power to change as much. Imagine the potential leverage of Europe had it teamed up to reduce this dependency.

Russia's war has already taught us: Waiting is not a good strategy. For years, European experts kept telling us that decoupling from Russian energy—and thus from Russia itself—wasn't an option. And just look where that has got us. The damage done to Germany, Europe, and the world is enormous. A study by the Brandenburg Institute for Society and Security entitled "The Price of Procrastination" ("Die Kosten des Zauderns") concludes that the Russian war of aggression is costing Germany around 200 billion euros a year—almost 6 percent of its economic output. According to the study, these costs consist mainly of a loss in economic growth due to the war (100 billion euros) and a reduction of inflation-adjusted net worth (70 billion euros). If we had invested earlier in reducing dependence on Russia, the costs would have been much lower. The study's authors point to a failed "appeasement policy" and summarize as follows: "Policies based on common fundamental values and ethical principles don't come for free. Lethargy, inertia, despondency, escapist self-delusion, and a psychological attachment to utopias result not only in moral but also financial costs. Appropriate defense through spending on civil, homeland, external, and cyber-security is the price of sustainable prosperity." The Basel Institute of Commons and Economics estimates that the costs of the Ukraine war for nonparticipants in the subsequent four years amount to around 2 trillion euros, of which 1.58 trillion euros are accounted for by the EU. Above all, higher energy costs are taking a major financial toll.

An orderly managed independence from Russia would have caused the EU, and especially Germany, significant hardship and losses in the short- to medium-term. Allowing the aggressor to determine events, however, has clearly turned out to be more painful. Not only is the economic damage of a completely different order, but there is an incalculable human cost to both sides.

This experience must make us realize that "business as usual" when dealing with China and other nondemocratic economies is the most dangerous solution of all. "Ostrich politics"—

sticking one's head in the sand—won't help. Neither will going off on one's own. The U.S. Inflation Reduction Act (IRA), for example, might be the largest law ever passed that secures national investments while addressing climate change, but so far it's also a failed attempt to unite the West. In securing domestic expenditure, the Inflation Reduction Act impacts not only current and future U.S. investments in China, but also those of democratic partner countries like France or Germany. The main reason for that failure is the unilateral approach in the IRA's implementation. When confronted with this outcome, there was criticism from the EU and its member countries. The IRA got portrayed as ruthless American protectionism. Instead, Europe could have done exactly the same, in a coordinated manner. In such a scenario, the Inflation Reduction Act would have been seen as a smart initiative of the transatlantic alliance to foster innovation and sustainability—and to strengthen democratic economies. It could truly have achieved what was defined as its original purpose for both sides of the Atlantic. A good example of why togetherness of democratic economies is mission critical in the defense of the open society model.

Creating a new trade architecture and redefining our relationship with autocracies wouldn't simply be a form of damage limitation. Taking these actions would also help us to avoid one of the biggest perils of our time, one which always arises from the "business as usual" strategy: progressive and dangerously escalating deglobalization. And with that, a new and lasting rise of nationalism.

Only when we proactively and jointly change our economic behavior and actions will democracies truly benefit. Only then will more and more countries join this alliance of truly free societies. Only then will there be increased international cooperation and a global pooling of interests. If we leave things up to the autocracies, we will either have to decouple abruptly at some point—or we will be cut loose, as is now the case with Russia. The upshot will be deglobalization. Globalization does not mean uniting everybody at once. Because if you unite too fast based on different standards, you provoke injustice and conflict. Globalization can only work in steps, based on mutual rules and standards and values.

Not every country will immediately wish or be able to escape the existing trade trap and join a new alliance of values and interests, but democracies would form the critical mass of an attractive trade order that draws in ever more countries. And at least this group of nations—which is still dominant in economic terms—would remain globalized, acting as a magnet that brings about not less but more international cooperation.

Some might say such an alliance restricts economic freedom. This argument is misleading. Business history is full of progress that, at a first glance, came across as limitations. Racial discrimination and gender equality were fiercely fought as an intrusion to economic freedom. That point was also made when sustainability targets were discussed. In the end, advanced standards have catalyzed innovation and accelerated value creation. And this will be even more true for a trade policy that is based on the universal values of freedom, rule of law, and human rights. It may feel uncomfortable at the beginning, but once we've taken the risk to try something new, we will reap the rewards. But we must prove the courage to give up a dysfunctional paradigm.

In May 2022, in light of the murderous war of Russia in Ukraine, NATO secretary general Jens Stoltenberg said: "Freedom is more important than free trade." This sentence captures the very essence of what is at stake—although I believe freedom and free trade are not alternatives to each other and should both be preserved. The key lies in redefining the concept of free trade. We need a new alliance engaged in truly free trade among democracies. Because we cannot trade freedom for profits. Or else we might lose both.

War, Peace, and My Father

I remember feeling ashamed of being German. At the age of sixteen, the TV miniseries Holocaust *showed me the horrors of National Socialism for the first time. It was 1979, and the images of the concentration camps, emaciated inmates, mountains of corpses, and the incredibly moving story of the Weiss family were all new to me. I didn't get how Germans could do such things, how they could want to do such things, or how they could have allowed it all to happen.*

My father, born in 1928, reinforced this sense of collective shame. He lived his life amid his memories of war. As a child he had been conscripted as a Flakhelfer to support the Luftwaffe, and as a teenager had to carry burned corpses out of bombed houses. At the end of the war, he was held in a French prisoner-of-war camp on the Atlantic coast. Sharing and remembering these experiences constantly brought him to tears. Using his hands to show us how small the burned corpses were after the bombings. Time and again, I heard him say: Germans started the war; nothing's more terrible than war; there must never be war again.

I was raised to be a pacifist, but never truly became one. It was clear to me the first time I delved into the history of the Third Reich that diplomacy, restraint, and messages of peace achieved nothing against dictators like Hitler. The appeasement policy of Neville Chamberlain—former prime minister of the United Kingdom—was a chilling and salutary example. How could anyone try to negotiate with someone like Hitler? Why didn't the Allies intervene earlier and more decisively? Why didn't they destroy the railroad tracks to the concentration camps? Millions of Jewish lives might have been saved. Millions of soldiers probably wouldn't have died. The bombing of Dresden, Rotterdam, and many other European cities might have been avoided. These are the lessons I drew from World War II: Racism, never again. Genocide, never again. Tolerance for intolerance, never again. Appeasement, never again.

My convictions were strengthened at the end of the Cold War. It wasn't peace speeches in Moscow or the recognition and glorification of the German Democratic Republic that brought down the Iron Curtain and the Berlin Wall. It was American deterrence backed by military strength, projects like the Strategic Defense Initiative and NATO's Double-Track Decision. And the courage of the people on the streets.

The end of the Cold War sparked my interest in politics— particularly the German reunification, which was its defining moment. The fall of the Berlin Wall was the iconic event of my generation. Before that, I wasn't particularly interested in the "other" Germany. My mother told me she felt more akin to Italians and the French than to her "German brothers and sisters" in Leipzig or Cottbus. It was the zeitgeist of the eighties.

But nevertheless, as I was sitting in front of a TV screen in Mu-

nich on November 9, 1989, watching the images of people knocking down the Berlin Wall and crossing the Brandenburg Gate, I was moved to tears. I realized that this revolution of the people was the ultimate triumph of freedom—the one thing worth defending and working for. That's why I moved to Berlin. And why I have never left.

PUTIN'S WAR AGAINST FREEDOM

In early 2022, Illia Bondarenko was a twenty-something young man, full of all the usual passion and plans, a talented violinist touring the world to pursue his dream of becoming a professional musician. Just the sort of young man who shouldn't have to worry about his family or friends, let alone his entire country. The courageous child of someone, born just a few weeks apart from my own son.

At the beginning of March, just two weeks after the Russian invasion of Ukraine, he found himself in a basement shelter in Kyiv while the city was being bombed. He started playing the violin in the gaps between the raids. One tune in particular stood out: the Ukrainian folk song *Verbovaya Doschechka*, which he performed, via the Internet, with over ninety violinists from twenty-nine countries—a gesture of solidarity, sharing a message of hope and support. I can still feel the goose bumps that watching the YouTube video gave me.

Vladimir Putin's assault on Ukraine has been ongoing since at least 2014. The annexation of Crimea was the first part of a long-term strategy that has two clear goals. The first is to restore the former superpower to its previous size and significance, following in the footsteps of role models like Peter the Great. It is likely that his plan is to target not only Ukraine, but also, in stages, the Baltic states, Poland, and other countries.

The second goal, perhaps even more important than the first, is the weakening of the West. Putin sees democracy as a degenerate concept undermining a nation's health and strength. The fact that ever more democracies are inching closer to Russia—thanks to the end of the Cold War and an expanded NATO—is viewed as a threat. Working in strategic synergy with China, Putin seeks to counter the danger of democratic subversion with a policy of autocratic strength and aggressive geopolitics.

Officially, the Cold War has been over for more than thirty years. This murky historical chapter, featuring numerous spies and a nuclear arms race, began shortly after World War II, and lasted until the fall of the Berlin Wall and the Iron Curtain. But for Putin, it never truly ended.

When Putin became president in 2000, he systematically developed a narrative that Mikhail Gorbachev's Perestroika and the 1991 August Coup, which helped Boris Yeltsin to seal his leadership, were a surrender to Western and especially United States policies. He himself—Vladimir Putin—would play a historic role in returning Russia to its old might and glory.

In this capacity, Putin acts like a scientist studying the West. He uses "lab experiments" to test reactions, probe limits, try out new methods, calculate probabilities, and forecast resilience. How strong, how weak, how united, or how divided are the EU, the United States, and the German-American axis? Influencing an election campaign through disinformation and bot-driven propaganda is as much a part of his methodology as a contract killing in the heart of Berlin or a war in Georgia. If the West reacts in a weak and divided way, he reads this as encouragement and proceeds to his next move. If the West reacts in an unexpectedly strong and united way, he pulls back, pauses, and reconsiders his options.

Europe has shown itself to be remarkably weak in the face of Putin's experimentation over the last twenty years: through its military passivity, through its pacifist obsession with principles, and especially through its decision to accelerate economic dependence on Russia. The war in the Caucasus in August 2008 was followed by a peace plan that was brokered by the European Council just days later. Putin saw this as encouragement. The Russian attack on Crimea in 2014 resulted in a de facto Russian incorporation of the peninsula, without resistance from the West. The events in Crimea delivered another positive lab result for this mad scientist. Putin understood that he could go further.

Simultaneously, there was a deepening economic dependence on Russia, particularly on the part of the largest EU member, Germany. In the aftermath of the Fukushima reactor disaster in Japan, Germany began phasing out nuclear power and steadily increasing its Russian gas imports, from around 36 percent in 2011 to 65 percent in 2020. Though, this growing relationship goes way back. According to *Der Spiegel*, in the beginning of Helmut Schmidt's chancellorship, 15 percent of Germany's gas imports came from Russia. A 30 percent rule limiting the amount of gas coming from a given country was installed under Schmidt to prevent the creation of dependencies. It was broken several years later under Helmut Kohl in 1991, when 33 percent of Germany's gas imports came from the Soviet Union. The completion of the Nord Stream 2 pipeline project, fast-tracked in spite of warnings from the United States, would have led to further direct dependence on Russia. In addition, around 40 percent of Germany's crude oil imports in January 2022 came from Russia. Even after the outbreak of war on February 24, 2022, the EU was still sending around $1 billion a day to Russia for energy imports. It was effectively financing Vladimir Putin's attempts to conquer Ukraine.

Energy dependency combined with a trade policy that was as shortsighted as it was naïve thus became the catalyst for military escalation, and led to a bitter awakening in Europe. Even the most cavalier advocates of apolitical trade policy (in line with the commonly known motto of American economist and Nobel Memorial Prize laureate Milton Friedman: "The purpose of business is business") have realized that trading with countries where the rule of law and human rights are trampled underfoot will sooner or later exact not only a high economic price, but an even higher political and humanitarian one. Ever since, global growth has slowed down. The consequences of a multinational recession and of inflation, significantly shaped by this war, can't even be quantified. Even less so its death toll.

In Germany, this conflict—so unexpected and unimaginable for many—was a shock and prompted an abrupt change in political direction. As the head of a coalition government made up, ironically, of the Greens, the liberal Free Democrats (FDP), and the Social Democrats (SPD), Chancellor Olaf Scholz adopted three measures that would have seemed unthinkable at any other point in the last fifteen years:

1. *A special budget of 100 billion euros to upgrade the German armed forces*

2. *A commitment to achieving NATO's target of spending 2 percent of GDP on defense*

3. *A pledge to supply Ukraine with weapons*

German foreign minister Annalena Baerbock, who had ruled out arms deliveries to Ukraine at the Munich Security Conference just days before Putin's attack, suddenly struck a completely different tone. In a special session of the Bundestag on February 27, 2022, referring to the lessons Germany had learned from National Socialism and the Holocaust, she said: "It may be that Germany is today leaving behind a special and unique form of restraint in foreign and security policy. The rules we set for ourselves must not mean that we cannot assume our responsibility. If our world is a different one, then our policy must also be different. . . . In keeping with our deepest convictions, we will continue to be cautious when it comes to arms exports and military operations. However, at this historic juncture, in the wake of this brutal attack against Ukraine, we will decide in favour of support to Ukraine that includes not only our large-scale economic and humanitarian engagement but also the supply of military material and weapons. Because we must not leave Ukraine defenceless against the aggressor bringing death and destruction to the country."

This was a second watershed moment: a historic adjustment of the special German path following a painful reality check. And it was set in motion by Germany's first female foreign minister, a member of the Greens, a party that had been founded on the twin

41

pillars of pacifism and withdrawal from nuclear energy. These two principles ended up clashing disastrously in the context of war, as it was the irrational fear of nuclear energy, above all else, that led to Germany's dependence on Putin's gas. This policy shift, under Chancellor Angela Merkel, shaped the Putin we're dealing with today. In this context, it is very telling how stubbornly the German government insisted on sticking to its plan of phasing out nuclear power plants—despite the severe energy crisis.

War is terrible and tragic. But Putin's attack on Ukraine and freedom had one indirectly positive effect: Opportunistic economic and trade policies lost their innocence. For business is never just business; it always involves more. And, in light of the Russian war against Ukraine and the Western values, business has never been so political. Even if a business wants to be and to act apolitical, almost everything it does or doesn't do has a political impact. Whether we like it or not, one purpose of business is politics. There is a growing realization around the world that when trade creates dependency, trouble will follow. Putin's war is a wake-up call for leaders and must presage a long overdue shift in the dynamic between economic policy and security policy, between democracies and dictatorships. And perhaps even more importantly, this war discredits appeasement once and for all—no matter how it is dressed up.

Back in 1999, it felt somehow liberating when another Green foreign minister, Joschka Fischer—influenced by the West's disgraceful failure to prevent the Srebrenica massacre in 1995—managed to push through the deployment of German soldiers in the Kosovo War. Fischer's justification was as clear as it was succinct: "I learned not just: 'Never again war.' I also learned: 'Never again Auschwitz.'" With German help, a barbarous conflict was ended not through passivity but through determined military intervention. There can be no tolerance for genocide.

When these debates started up again around the world in 2022, following the invasion of Ukraine, it was interesting to see the fault lines emerge. Outrage about arms deliveries to Ukraine came mostly from countries or sections of society that were living in peace and guaranteed prosperity, and whose only contact with totalitarian behavior was via history books or on television. Conversely, many countries and societies that had been forced to fight for their freedom or were still having to fight for it, or that had direct experience of dictators and Russian aggression, were in favor of military intervention. Ideology or party allegiances hardly played any role. Almost as many senior politicians in the Green Party supported a policy of military solidarity as those in the more conservative Christian Democrat Union (CDU).

There is an eternal conflict between "doves" and "hawks." Doves believe the best way to avoid or end wars is through restraint, keeping out of things, offering compromises, always talking. Hawks believe that the best way to avoid and end conflicts is through deterrence, strength, and a mixture of credible threats and diplomacy.

Of course, we would all rather be doves. But history has shown us that the "hawks" have got it right when it comes to securing or restoring peace. That's how it was in World War II, which only ended through the courageous actions of the Allies. Or in the Yom Kippur War, where American military support for Israel led to the signing of a cease-fire. Or in the Kosovo War, which only ended following NATO intervention.

In all of these cases, further escalation was a risk. And this risk was cited yet again as the reason for non-intervention in the Ukraine war.

The escalation-avoidance theory is based on a false assumption: that autocratic or dictatorial aggressors will be satisfied if they are allowed to achieve their initial goal. There is very little evidence to support this in Putin's case. It was just this kind of naïveté that allowed him to annex Crimea in 2014. He drew just one conclusion from it all: Escalate further.

What if Putin now attacks the Baltic states or perhaps even Poland? Then—as per Article 5 of the NATO treaty—the alliance would be formally obliged to intervene. But would the argument for avoiding escalation at all costs then no longer apply?

Perhaps one would have to say: The risk of further escalation is too great, we can't risk a nuclear war for a tiny set of Baltic states. And what if a dictator like Putin uses poison gas or tactical nuclear weapons one day, if chemical or biological weapons cause terrible casualties, and images are beamed around the world that exceed our worst imaginings? Would the West really still not intervene? Would it continue to maintain a cautious stance in order to prevent worse escalation? The problem with this kind of strategy is that, with every passing week, the number of victims increases, and so does the level of violence deployed.

If one takes the escalation-avoidance argument seriously, there's just one logical step: the swiftest possible capitulation. This would apply to Syria and Afghanistan, to Israel, and one day to Taiwan. Only swift capitulation would avert many thousands of deaths, saving the lives of soldiers and civilians—especially children—from Russia and Ukraine, from the Baltic states and Poland, from Israel and Taiwan. It would be a terrible choice, but an honest one at least. It would mean surrendering our values.

Germany's stubbornness in refusing to provide decisive assistance for too long reveals a certain callousness: "Sorry. Not our responsibility. We can't help." But how would Germany feel if a dictator attacked Berlin, and its ally America said: "So sorry, there's nothing we can do, the risk of escalation is simply too high."

One recent symbolic instance of German aloofness came on March 17, 2022—the somber day when the president of Ukraine, Volodymyr Zelenskyy, asked the German Bundestag for assistance. His heartfelt speech was received with some emotion, after which it was business as usual, including the reading out of birthday greetings. Impact? Zero. Help? None. Not without some bitterness, the courageous Ukrainian president summed up the German position thus: "I appeal to you on behalf of everyone who has heard politicians say: 'Never again.' And who saw that these words are worthless."

It was on that day that I began to fear we Germans were squandering the second chance we had been given after 1945. In Mariupol, homes were burning, people were starving; men were being strip-searched by Russian soldiers, civilians deliberately shot, children murdered; bodies were lying in the streets. And we Germans didn't see any of it as our responsibility. Germany is the world champion in *Gratis Mut*—the empty courage that incurs no risks. The art of taking riskless risks.

The footage from Ukraine is deeply moving. Soldiers in combat gear in Odesa playing "Don't Worry, Be Happy" in front of their military barricades. Illia Bondarenko playing a Ukrainian folk song in a bunker in Kyiv together with violinists from all over the world. These are gestures of strength and solidarity, in the most emotional and universal language of the world: music. But music alone won't do it. And, despite all, that's something even Germany has fortunately come to realize—late, but not too late.

Staging Power—
How to Recognize Autocrats

As the CEO of a publishing company, I've met with many politicians over the years—democratic ones and not so democratic ones. I've had many conversations with Helmut Kohl, Gerhard Schröder, Angela Merkel, and Olaf Scholz. And, with the exception of Donald Trump, I've met every former American president of the past few decades, starting with George H. W. Bush.

The funniest and most surprising encounter I ever had with a head of state was with George W. Bush. Henry Kissinger had suggested that if I would like to meet him, I should get my assistant to pass on my next United States travel dates. Which she did, including a trip to a Time Warner board meeting just two days later. That evening, on the French Atlantic coast, I got an email from the White House: The president would be delighted to meet me the day after tomorrow, July 25, 2007, at 9:30 a.m. in the Oval Office. Not only was I amazed at the speed with which the meeting had been scheduled, I was also in the depths of rural France—and logistically challenged. First, there was no connecting flight that could get me to Washington on time. Second, my eleven-year-old son was with me and I had promised that he could come to New York this time. In a cloak-and-dagger operation, my office organized a private plane which picked us up on the runway of Angoulême-Cognac Airport the following day and dropped us off in Washington nine hours later. On the way from the airport to the White House, I called the president's assistant and asked where I could leave my son during the meeting. Bring him along, she said kindly. He can hang out with me and shoot the breeze about basketball.

Once we were at the White House, everything happened very quickly. Suddenly, I was sitting in the most famous office in the world. On a sofa. Across from the 43rd President of the United States of America. Two ladies with notepads were also in attendance. Do we need note takers, Bush asked, laughing, crinkling his eyes. I shook my head. You ladies can go, you're on break now, he called out with a smile. For half an hour, we talked, completely alone, about the next American election. To my surprise Bush was quite convinced that Hillary Clinton would be his successor: And I reckon she won't do badly at all, he said, with more continuity in foreign policy than many might think. George Bush was surprisingly easygoing, approachable, not at all aloof, quite different from what I had expected, with a quick acumen and sparky humor. What surprised me most was his honesty and a startling willingness to be self-critical. How did he cope with all the media criticism without becoming bitter? He gave a levelheaded answer: I'm criticized for mistakes we made in Iraq. I have to take responsibility for those myself, so I can't blame the journalists. After half an hour, he said: Let's go get a photo with your son, and then I'll have to move on.

Never has the media-generated image I had of a person contrasted so sharply with the impression I gained through a direct encounter. I met a president who acknowledged that the Iraq war was based on false assumptions, a president who had limited individual freedoms in the name of a war of terror, and a president who was ridiculed by the media for his sloppy communication style. But the president I met in person was the antithesis of the president I thought I already knew. And neither before nor since have I met a top politician who was so authentic, unpretentious, and down to earth in his role as the elected representative of the people. This wasn't a power-hungry man, but rather a servant of democracy.

A few years earlier, on July 9, 2004, my visit to Downing Street for an exploratory chat with Tony Blair played out in a similar way. The Axel Springer publishing group was in the advanced stages of a bidding war for The Daily Telegraph, *the long-established British newspaper. It seemed sensible for us to call on the British prime minister—to get a feel for whether a German owner might meet some political resistance in the UK.*

Number 10—as the British call their prime minister's HQ— is the opposite of an imposing or luxurious residence. You go in through the front door as if you were popping round to see a neighbor. The walls haven't been decorated for a while; here and there old nails stick out of the wallpaper where pictures used to hang. Everything from the furniture to the dim lamps has a shabby-chic charm that sends out two messages: (1) We maintain tradition here, and (2) we don't waste taxpayers' money. Fittingly, when I enter his office, the prime minister is at his desk wearing a blue shirt with both sleeves rolled up. The guest is invited to remove his jacket too. Here, proximity is cultivated over distance and authority. Less a staging of power than a staging of powerlessness. Civility as a leading principle. One sovereign entity, the state, facing another sovereign entity, the citizen, at eye level.

We chat about German politics and the British media. Blair jokes about the journalists who mock him for being Bush's poodle and explains what riles him most about the British tabloid press. But then adds: That's just the way things are here. Toward the end of our meeting, I steer the conversation round to my questions: Would we be welcome in the UK? Does he think there might be political pushback? Each time, the prime minister tells me that he doesn't have the authority to say. He himself would welcome a German owner, but there might still be some difficulties: Politics is unpredictable and the party landscape diverse. He really couldn't say, he really didn't know. The conversation ends in a friendly fashion with no clear outcome. A few weeks later, when another bidder makes a much higher offer for The Daily Telegraph *and we're out of the running, I feel sad. We would have felt at home in the UK.*

Our experience in Turkey tells a different story. Aydın Doğan is a proud man with thick, glossy black hair. He was once Turkey's biggest media entrepreneur. His empire included the most influential Turkish daily newspaper, Hürriyet; *the largest Turkish daily newspaper,* Posta; *the most influential political TV station,* CNN Türk; *private TV station* Kanal D; *and numerous other media outlets. We've known each other for a long time, not least because his company had a German printing plant that printed some of our newspapers for years. Doğan was a reliable business partner, but the Doğan Media Group also impressed me as a whole, because their editorial teams advocated a strict separation between state and religion, and—in keep-*

ing with the tradition of Turkey's former president Kemal Atatürk—a modern, moderate form of Islam. His media outlets encouraged their readers and viewers to live a free lifestyle, and viewed the headscarf as a symbol of women's oppression. It was a media company that stood for modern Turkey.

Doğan was financially successful and his company's values matched those of Axel Springer. Both of us had big ambitions. And so, from 2003 onward, we repeatedly discussed taking major growth steps together. We thought Axel Springer buying a minority stake in Doğan could be a good first step.

We were explicitly encouraged by the Turkish government. Prime Minister Recep Tayyip Erdoğan, who had been in office since 2003, gave us repeated, personal encouragement. I met three times with Turkey's new strongman, who was considered a reformer at the beginning of the millennium. The first time was in a hotel in Istanbul, where we discussed German-Turkish friendship and Erdoğan's blood pressure problems. Then there was a secret meeting in a government building, which my colleagues and I were obliged to access through a back entrance. Erdoğan was seen as a modernizer, as someone whose thinking was less traditional than what he actually said, and above all, as a close friend of Aydın Doğan. He gave his wholehearted support to Axel Springer investing in Turkey. He was highly engaged and keen to persuade us to enter the partnership.

The high point of the charm offensive was a meeting at Ankara Airport on March 10, 2005. We were told that this meeting was of the highest priority for the Turkish prime minister and could only be held at that place and time. I was happy to oblige. After all, an investment of a few hundred million euros was on the line, and *there were some antitrust obstacles, as foreigners could only hold a stake of up to 25 percent according to Turkish law—although a change to that law was under discussion.*

We were received by Erdoğan and his large entourage in a special lounge at the airport. A single scene from this discussion stands out in my memory. There was some uncertainty about the interpretation of the law, and our lawyers had doubts about whether the deal could be approved. The prime minister listened attentively and then pulled out his cell phone. Several calls, loud voice, sweeping hand gestures. After ten minutes, the matter was settled. Don't worry, he said, you won't have any problems. It was very clear who was the boss here. While impressed by Erdoğan's intervention and speediness, I was also a bit skeptical about the reliability of these assurances. Not least because of this, we agreed onto a value guarantee for our entire investment. Secured by a bank guarantee, the value of our shares could from now on never fall below the entry price. This clause has saved us hundreds of millions of euros in Turkey. Why? Because the cordial relationship between Prime Minister (later President) Erdoğan and media entrepreneur Aydın Doğan deteriorated for inexplicable reasons. Perhaps because the Turkish owner and his German partner were serious about maintaining editorial independence in Turkey? Initially a liberalizer, Erdoğan became increasingly less democratic and more hard-line. Years of litigation followed. An alleged tax offense led to a ruinous fine of over two and a half billion dollars for Doğan. In March 2014, a phone call was made public in which Erdoğan instructed his minister of justice to make sure Doğan received a harsh court judgment. At that point, I learned an enduring lesson: that it is not a good sign when heads of state show their strength. And that it is better when politicians say: I'm afraid I can't help.

Many years later, in a somewhat ironic postscript, Erdoğan, of all people, sued me twice in Germany—and lost—because I sided with a German comic who had offended the Turkish president. This was about the law and the right to satirical freedom of expression, which, in a democracy, even an autocrat from Turkey can't limit or question.

In my conversations with democratic leaders over the years, the desire to proclaim the limits of their power has been a common feature. It's nice of you to ask, but I'm afraid I can't help you there. Autocrats, on the other hand, are characterized by the constant desire to proclaim their power. Proudly demonstrating the leader's unique and ultimate authority is very much the hallmark of the despot. Strongmen brag with strength, democrats demonstrate understatement—as a proof of respect for democratic institutions.

PART II

THE PROBLEM: FREEDOM IS FRAGILE

RULE BY FEAR

While democratic countries weaken themselves from within, either through populism or the lame leadership of opportunistic centrist governments, autocracies and absolute dictatorships continue to gain in strength. This is partly due to their economic success, and partly to the increasingly uninhibited oppression of their own people or horrific displays of intolerance—often both at once. Freedom of expression, especially in the media, is front and center here. Restrictions on press freedom remain the clearest indicator of a country's lack of freedom. The erosion of freedom of expression and the rule of law, and a disregard for human rights, usually run very much in tandem. Evan Gershkovich's case is only the latest of a long list of wrongfully incarcerated journalists. The *Wall Street Journal* reporter was jailed in Russia in late March 2023 on charges of espionage—the first U.S. journalist to be detained for spying since the end of the Cold War.

Whether it's Russia or China; Turkey or Belarus; Qatar or Saudi Arabia; Syria, Afghanistan, or Iran: Discrimination, homophobia, the violation of women's rights, and aggressive curbs on opposition are on the rise. And because the media cannot operate freely in these autocratic or totalitarian states, their misdeeds are not publicly exposed.

Freedom of expression and media freedom are in significant decline around the world. According to the organization Reporters Without Borders, press freedom is in a difficult or very grave state in 73 of the 180 countries it surveyed, and is facing visible difficulties in 55 others. Independent journalism is thus considerably restricted in nearly three-quarters of all countries. At the beginning of December 2022, a total of 363 journalists were held in prisons globally, according to the Committee to Protect Journalists (CPJ). That is substantially more than in previous years, and the highest figure since the turn of the millennium—at that point it was 99 reporters. Topping the somber leader board with 62 imprisoned journalists is Iran. China, Myanmar (Burma), and Turkey are behind. Their "crimes" are effectively independent reporting and being critical of the government.

The methods employed by such states are increasingly unscrupulous. On May 23, 2021, a Ryanair flight from Athens to Vilnius was forced to make an emergency landing in Belarus due to a suspected bomb. On the orders of Belarusian dictator Alexander Lukashenko, fighter jets escorted the passenger plane to the ground. On board were Belarusian journalist Raman Pratasevich and his Russian girlfriend Sofia Sapega. Both were arrested after the flight touched down. Pratasevich had repeatedly voiced criticism of the Belarusian regime over the years, both as editor of the Warsaw-based news channel Nexta and as an independent blogger with rapidly growing reach. The whereabouts of Pratasevich and Sapega were initially unclear. It was not until the following day that Belarusian state media released a video of Pratasevich saying that he was fine and being treated well. Bruises could be seen on his face in the recording. Despite other videos featuring Pratasevich, in which he said he was in good health and praised the regime, observers believed he was being tortured and forced to confess on camera. He was released under house arrest in June 2021 and apparently freed half a year later. He pleaded guilty, was sentenced to eight years' imprisonment in a "trial" in 2023, and was pardoned shortly thereafter by Lukashenko himself.

This case has added a new dimension to the way regimes aggressively attack freedom of expression and human rights, because Pratasevich was not apprehended in Belarus, but simply when flying over its territory. It means that not only will journalists, civil rights activists, and regime opponents need to think carefully about which countries they actually visit in future, but anyone flying over the Middle East may soon have reason to feel very anxious when their plane enters Iran or Saudi airspace. What Lukashenko and other autocrats are concerned with here, in addition to suppressing undesirable information and opinions, is intimidation. For centuries, fear has been one of the most efficient means of consolidating totalitarian power.

North Korea—old-style dictatorship par excellence—doesn't even care about making a positive impression. Basic human rights, freedom of opinion, and press freedom are all denied here. For decades, the Communist leadership has starved its own people, and now it regularly provokes the West with nuclear weapon tests. These days, the regime's human rights crimes against its own people attract hardly any attention—it's only when foreign nationals are affected that the world occasionally looks up. The case of Otto Warmbier caused a wave of international outrage.

The American student was arrested at Pyongyang Airport in 2016 for allegedly stealing a propaganda poster. He admitted the crime at a press conference, but may well have been under duress. Warmbier was sentenced to fifteen years in a labor camp for this "theft." In June 2017, he was flown back to the United States in a coma. The twenty-two-year-old died of severe brain injuries a few days later. The official North Korean explanation was that Warmbier had suffered an episode of food poisoning along with an adverse reaction to a sleeping pill. His parents refused an autopsy. Since then, this brave couple has campaigned for human rights to be observed internationally.

As rogue states go, Iran is only a step or two behind North Korea. Since the mullahs seized power at the end of the 1970s, the country has abandoned all democratic values and isolated itself politically to a large extent. Women's rights are virtually nonexistent, and anyone not living according to the regime's tenets risks death. In September 2022, a twenty-two-year-old woman was beaten by the morality police for not wearing her hijab correctly. She died of suspicious circumstances while in police custody. The killing of Mahsa Amini led to nationwide protests that sparked global solidarity. As a sign of their anger against the mullahs' regime, women have burned their hijabs and cut their hair. A few years earlier, in 2016, Iranian-Swedish scientist Ahmadreza Djalali was arrested in Iran and sentenced to death the following year. He had been accused of passing information about Iran's nuclear program to Israel. Photos allegedly showing Djalali with Israeli spies were submitted as evidence, but those "spies" turned out to be Italian doctors. For years, Djalali has woken every morning knowing that this could be the day he is executed. His wife and children have fought desperately for his release. Human rights organizations speak of a politically motivated trial. Iran, they say, wants to secure the release of an Iranian spy imprisoned in Sweden.

Writer Salman Rushdie is another of Iran's prominent victims. He was stabbed by a man of Lebanese descent during a reading in Chautauqua, in Upstate New York, on August 12, 2022. Badly wounded, Rushdie was quickly taken to a hospital and survived, but he has lost the sight in one eye and the use of a hand. It was the culmination of an unparalleled campaign to hunt down the Indian-British writer. "I am informing all brave Muslims of the world that the author of *The Satanic Verses*, a text written, edited, and published against Islam, the Prophet of Islam, and the Qu'ran, along with all the editors and publishers aware of its contents, are condemned to death. I call on all valiant Muslims wherever they may be in the world to kill them without delay, so that no one will dare insult the sacred beliefs of Muslims henceforth. Whoever is killed in this cause will be a martyr, God Willing." With these words in 1989, Iran's former leader, Ayatollah Ruhollah Khomeini, called for the killing of the writer, shortly after the publication of *The Satanic Verses*. According to extremist Muslims, the book insults the Prophet Muhammad. Iran has even placed a bounty on the writer's head. Rushdie's death is worth more than $3.9 million: $3.3 million from the state-run 15 Khordad Foundation and another $600,000 from a consortium of 40 Iranian state-run news outlets. In 2007, protests erupted in Iran and Pakistan after Rushdie received a knighthood from the Queen. A Pakistani minister said this honor justified suicide bombings. Following the 2022 attempt on the author's life, *Kayhan*, a newspaper close to the regime, whose editor is personally appointed by the head of state, praised "the brave and dutiful person who attacked the apostate and evil Salman Rushdie in New York. . . . The hand of the man who tore the neck of God's enemy must be kissed." Headlines sounded like "Satan on the Road to Hell"—and there was reference to an "arrow" shot by Ayatollah Khomeini, which would one day hit its target.

One totalitarian regime linked to the United States on several levels—energy, security, intelligence—is Saudi Arabia. These links are understandable and reasonable if it is about the support and right of existence of the state of Israel. Beyond that, these are possibly short-sighted, as Saudi Arabia—a pure-play autocracy—is increasingly leaning toward China, both politically and culturally. While being critical of the Biden administration, Crown Prince Mohammed bin Salman has also copied Xi Jinping's tactics: suppressing political dissent, focusing on economic growth, and pursuing a self-serving foreign policy. China has already become Saudi Arabia's most important strategic partner, because it is the latter's largest oil trading partner. This strategic importance is reflected in the fact that Saudi secondary schools have begun to teach Chinese. America nevertheless intensifies its friendly relationship with Saudi Arabia because the enemy of our enemy (Iran and others) is our friend (while ignoring that it is also the friend of an even bigger foe). And because of the very—perhaps too—pragmatic advantages that this relationship provides economically and with regard to intelligence cooperation, security policy, and foreign policy in the Middle East. That policy has been proved wrong many times, with Iran and Iraq and a couple of other friendly foes and false friends. A policy that allows cooperation on a strategic level with regard to Israel's protection remains desirable. A trade policy that leads to dependency in certain areas seems dangerous on many levels and in a very concrete sense.

Jamal Khashoggi's assassination has become the world's

most infamous symbol of brutal human rights violations aimed at media intimidation. The foreign correspondent, who worked for the *Washington Post* and other publications, was killed in an unprecedented attack at the Saudi consulate in Istanbul, where he was collecting the documents he needed for his marriage. A U.N. investigation has concluded that his murder was organized by the Saudi state. This report also reveals how meticulously and deceitfully Khashoggi's October 2, 2018, killing was planned. In the morning, a fifteen-strong murder squad, some of whom had arrived on a private jet, asked staff to leave the consulate. A surveillance video shows Khashoggi innocently entering the building. The audio recordings that captured what followed are almost unbearable. After a gruesome struggle, the body of the murdered man was probably dismembered. The whole process was reminiscent of a ritual slaughter—the killers acted like butchers, in a cold and unusually savage manner. Shortly afterward, a number of vehicles left the consulate. To this day, the whereabouts of Khashoggi's body remain unknown. After issuing denials for weeks, Saudi Arabia finally admitted to the murder on October 19, but there has been no real fallout for the gulf state. Meanwhile, Saudi Arabia has sought to distract attention from its violation of fundamental human rights by investing heavily in the Western world, for example in soccer, the "beautiful game" adored throughout Europe. While there were only a few small demonstrations and protests after Khashoggi's murder, thousands of fans took to the streets in sheik costumes to celebrate the takeover of England's Newcastle United Football Club by the Saudi sovereign Public Investment Fund (PIF). Sportswashing works.

Homosexuality is a crime in Saudi Arabia, punishable by the

lash, imprisonment, or even the death penalty. The Committee for the Propagation of Virtue and Prevention of Vice, a kind of religious police, monitors social life. Islamic religious police are as active on streets and in homes as they are on the Internet.

People are still prosecuted for same-sex sexual activity in sixty-nine countries in the world, and in eleven of these it is punishable by death.

We pay great attention to every last nuance of diversity sensitivity in America and Europe so as not to exclude any sexual identity; almost every company has diversity officers dedicated to the goals of the LGBTQIA+ movement. We discuss whether public figures should resign if they forget to mention a particular minority during a speech at an event. And at the same time, we happily do business with countries where people are killed for being gay.

Autocracies and dictatorships are on the offensive worldwide. Democracies and open societies are on the defensive. Weak centrist politicians and strong, unscrupulous populists have precipitated a deep crisis in the values of open societies. And a well-intentioned "woke" culture war movement is employing increasingly intolerant methods in the name of noble humanitarian goals. The consequences are an iconoclasm reminiscent of the Middle Ages, a power struggle akin to the French Revolution, and restrictions on thought and speech that echo dictatorships of the recent European past—all of which threaten freedom. While the crimes of slavery are finally undergoing historical reassessment, democracy is embarking on a new kind of enslavement. It is the enslavement of the free mind to authoritarian thought patterns, and thus in the long run the capitulation of open societies to authoritarian regimes.

This process of enslavement is happening from below and above.

From below: We see a human rights and citizens' movement whose culture wars in the name of tolerance involve a highly intolerant reassessment of values. The honeypots of privilege, wealth, and power are to be redistributed. Minorities will determine for themselves when they have been discriminated against and by whom—a subjective sense of injustice and a fight against power abuse that is now itself being used as a power play. Punishments and rewards are to be randomly dispensed by those affected: the self-declared victims. As is so often the case, after centuries of dominant, inhumane patriarchies, the pendulum has now swung too far in the other direction—toward an equally intolerant minority abuse of power.

From above: We see the rise of the strong authoritarian leader. From Xi in China to Putin in Russia, from Assad in Syria to Kim in North Korea, dictators are ruthlessly implementing their plans. From Erdoğan in Turkey to Ahmadinejab, Rohani, or now Raisi in Iran, autocrats are playing cat and mouse with a naïve Western world. And from Poland to Hungary, populists have been coercing their EU partners, emboldened by sometimes clownish contributions from the heads of two of the world's most important and stable democracies—Great Britain and America. Even in Israel—democracy's bridgehead in the Middle East—a judiciary reform plan has harmed the reputation and credibility of a rules-based system. Globally, there is just one recognizable trend: the rise of the authoritarian politician.

As Gideon Rachman summarizes in his book *The Age of the Strongman*: "Since 2000 the rise of the strongman leader has become a central feature of global politics. In capitals as diverse as

Moscow, Beijing, Delhi, Ankara, Budapest, Warsaw, Manila, Riyadh and Brasilia, self-styled 'strongmen' (and, so far, they are all men) have risen to power. Typically, these leaders are nationalists and cultural conservatives, with little tolerance for minorities, dissent or the interests of foreigners. At home, they claim to be standing up for the common man against the 'globalist' elites. Overseas, they posture as the embodiment of their nations. And, everywhere they go, they encourage a cult of personality."

Fear is the strongman's tool and is thus the weapon of the hour. Fear was also used as a political lever in the fight against COVID-19. Health and security have always been the promise of authoritarian regimes, and now these are being promised to open societies, which are willing for their sake to sacrifice many of the basic freedoms they take for granted. Restrictions on freedom are thus being applied from the outside, from above, but also from within and from below. And of course the strength of an authoritarian leader is always linked to the weakness of his counterparts in established institutions within the democratic system. It was decades of decline in the quality, authenticity, and leadership abilities of the average politician from big, established parties that facilitated this development in the first place.

The two biggest challenges of our time act like catalysts in this situation: China's new role as a world power, which will lead not only to economic dominance but to extensive political influence as well, and the consequences of climate change, which may trigger not only mass migrations and societal shifts, but also an erosion of freedom that is driven from within.

In his book, Rachman comes to an optimistic conclusion about the future of democracy: "Democratic systems, for all their weaknesses, have institutions and laws that manage the crucial and delicate problem of succession. Durable political systems ultimately rely on institutions, not individuals. And successful societies are built on laws rather than charismatic leadership. For all these reasons, strongman rule is an inherently flawed and unstable form of government. It will ultimately collapse in China and in most other places where it is tried. But there may be a lot of turmoil and suffering before the Age of the Strongman is finally consigned to history."

He may be right. But none of this will come about of its own accord. Passivity won't stop climate policies restricting freedoms and progress any more than it will stop China's aggressive economic and political infiltration of free societies. In order to keep the turmoil and suffering which Rachman references as brief and as minimal as possible, we need decisive action.

In the past, business leaders have not pushed for necessary change, but mostly spoiled it. Too many cared too little about the political consequences. That changes if things switch from the political to the personal.

Unfortunately, the attitude of many business managers who defend doing business with dictators often only changes if they are themselves suddenly exposed to existential risks and threats. What the absence of the rule of law means remains an abstract idea until you have experienced it yourself. Leaders who used to make jokes of colleagues who expressed fears about autocratic regimes changed their tone and actions swiftly after they experienced or witnessed a case themselves—a colleague who was shot, a friend who got kidnapped, a family member who was sentenced to jail without any trial or judicial reason.

A good way to avoid your own real-life experience of deterrence is the book *Red Notice* by Bill Browder, in which the author tells his own story. For a few years around the turn of the millennium, Browder was a very successful fund manager in Russia—seemingly benefiting from the system. After a prosperous start, he became vocal about and active against the fraud and illegal behavior of the Russian political and business elites—until one day in 2005 when he was detained at the Russian customs without reason and, after a day of existential terror, was expelled from Russia and sent back to London. This was the beginning of a brutal fight, during which many people suffered. In 2009, one of Browder's lawyers, Sergei Magnitsky, was tortured and killed in a Russian prison, for no reason except working and defending the interests of an unwelcome businessman. This traumatic experience turned the former "pragmatist" and biggest foreign investor in Russia into a restless human rights activist who has since changed U.S. legislation.

Perhaps that's the clearer message for opportunistic managers: Business in nondemocratic countries can be deadly.

Imprisoned for
Reporting the Truth

At the Axel Springer headquarters in Berlin, we would frequently discuss whether it was still a good idea for Deniz Yücel, one of our WELT correspondents, to be based in Turkey. We were concerned by the Turkish government's increasingly hostile response to critical reporting—including that of foreign media—and we knew that Yücel's dual German-Turkish citizenship made him more vulnerable to the capriciousness of Turkish law than colleagues of a different nationality. WELT editor Ulf Poschardt raised these issues with his reporter numerous times. But Deniz insisted that he felt safe and that he was determined to stay on in Turkey.

In February 2017, like many other journalists, Deniz had reported on the leaked emails of Energy Minister Berat Albayrak, who also happens to be President Erdoğan's son-in-law. After learning that the police were looking for him, Deniz initially took refuge in a German embassy compound. But this hiding place and the very act of hiding became increasingly problematic for him, as it might be publicly interpreted as an admission of guilt. Normal reporting activities aside, Deniz's conduct has been beyond reproach. And surely, most of us reason, the Turkish government won't throw an internationally renowned journalist into prison before the eyes of the world just because of some critical reporting. But this move— Deniz handing himself in to the police—turns out to be a mistake. He is detained due to "terrorist propaganda." A court authorizes pretrial detention, which in Turkey can last up to five years. If convicted, he faces up to eighteen years in prison.

The news is a bombshell. Over in Berlin we reproach ourselves bitterly. Should we have acted more decisively and recalled our correspondent—even against his will? Yes, say some. No, say others: Deniz knew the danger he was putting himself in; he knowingly took that risk so he could keep reporting on the problematic developments in his country. The truth is: Journalism is dangerous. And if we were to recall independent journalists whenever things got tricky or dangerous, then the enemies of freedom would triumph, and the law of the strongest and most ruthless would win out.

The same goes for our war reporters. At times, we had more than twenty war reporters reporting from Ukraine and Russia. They risk their lives every single day. For us, it's vital that no one feels pressured into going, that our journalists head off on their assignments as thoroughly prepared as possible, that we support them with the best security measures—and that ideally they have no small children. Journalism, if you take it seriously, is unfortunately life-threatening, especially when you need it the most. That's when those subjected to its gaze find it especially unwelcome.

After a couple of weeks, Deniz is transferred to a maximum security prison. From this point onward, he sits in solitary confinement without a formal charge. He describes his prison conditions in a message to the WELT editorial team: "Being constantly alone is almost a kind of torture. All I can see through the window is a 6-meter-high wall. My only view of the sky is through the barbed wire on top of the wall." In addition to being suspected of terrorism, he's now also accused of sedition, because he once interviewed a senior member of the Kurdistan Workers' Party (PKK).

President Erdoğan publicly accuses Deniz of espionage and describes him as a German agent. German politicians from Chancellor Angela Merkel to Finance Minister Wolfgang Schäuble and newly elected President Frank-Walter Steinmeier call for Deniz's release.

In April, Deniz marries his girlfriend Dilek Mayatürk. As his wife, she is allowed to visit him in prison for one hour a week. She regularly shows him letters from concerned WELT readers, who encourage him to stay strong. He reports being subjected to psychological terror and mild forms of physical torture. Through conversations with his wife, I get a sense how bad things are for Deniz. His physical and mental health are clearly deteriorating. WELT sets up an email account where readers can send Deniz their messages.

Three hundred days after his arrest, Deniz writes an article about his life behind bars. Using the reverse of the newspaper pages, readers can lay out the actual size of Deniz's cell on the floor. It is tiny. 13.7 by 10.2 feet. Oppressive even without walls. Several celebrities take part in a coordinated call for Deniz's release. Among them are well-known musicians like Bono and Sting, the film directors Wim Wenders and Fatih Akın, and Nobel literature laureate Herta Müller.

Through Turkish and German lawyers, Deniz files a complaint with the European Court of Human Rights. As a way of increasing *pressure we decide to file a separate complaint with the court for violation of press freedom.*

Demonstrations calling for Deniz Yücel's release are held in Berlin and other German cities. We feel torn. On the one hand, these are heartfelt humanitarian gestures. On the other, the publicity may make it harder to find a face-saving solution in Turkey. But we can't change or influence these events anyway. Behind the scenes, we explore every possible way of helping Deniz. We turn to our contacts in the German, American, and Israeli embassies, which have traditionally had close diplomatic contacts with the Turkish government. Through official and unofficial political channels, I mobilize every conceivable form of help, and sense an unusually high level of engagement. Alongside Foreign Minister Sigmar Gabriel, who works on the issue almost daily, former German Chancellor Gerhard Schröder offers his support, flying twice to Istanbul to negotiate with President Erdoğan. In December, Deniz is released from solitary confinement. There is media speculation that Sigmar Gabriel has offered to supply weapons to Turkey in exchange for his release. Deniz makes it clear that he does not want to be part of a possible arms deal between Germany and Turkey. Gabriel confirms that there was and is no link to any arms deliveries.

In February, almost exactly a year after Deniz's arrest, German Chancellor Angela Merkel appeals for his release at a meeting with Turkish Prime Minister Binali Yıldırım. A day later, Deniz is released from prison—after 368 days in custody. In a video message, he says: "Just as my arrest had nothing to do with law and order, so my release has nothing to do with them either."

That afternoon, Sigmar Gabriel and I hold a press conference in the WELT newsroom. Statesmanlike words from the foreign minister. Aside from expressing my thanks and my relief, words largely fail me. Almost the entire editorial team is present, and many colleagues have tears in their eyes. On the evening of February 16, 2018, Deniz lands at Berlin's Tegel Airport. When he returns to the newsroom on March 19, the applause lasts for minutes.

In July 2020, Deniz Yücel is sentenced in absentia to two years, nine months and twenty-two days by the Turkish authorities—for spreading propaganda. In May 2023, an Istanbul-based court issues a new arrest warrant for Deniz. We call his real crime something else: the dissemination of uncomfortable truths.

Over the years, our colleagues have repeatedly been placed in life-threatening situations or fallen victim to authoritarian power—either for publishing uncomfortable truths or as a way of preventing their publication. One of our most challenging cases next to Deniz Yücel began unfolding in October 2010. Marcus Hellwig, a reporter for BILD, our biggest German media brand, had traveled to Iran on a tourist visa with his photographer Jens Koch. It was the only way they could enter the country to research a particularly delicate story: that of Sakineh Mohammadi Ashtiani, a forty-three-year-old mother who had been sentenced to death by stoning for allegedly committing adultery. Later, she was also accused of being involved in the murder of her husband.

To investigate this case, our journalists meet with Ashtiani's lawyer and son. In the course of the interview, all four are arrested. Marcus and Jens are then accused of entering Iran on a tourist visa despite intending to carry out journalistic work.

During the initial period of imprisonment, Marcus is kept in a single cell of around sixty-five square feet in size. The light is kept on the whole time. He is forced to wear a blindfold, to prevent him knowing what's going on around him.

After forty-three days in detention, the two still have no law-

yer. Representatives from the German embassy in Tehran are given little access to the detainees. For a long period, diplomatic efforts and public appeals are unsuccessful. Feverishly, we look for solutions. Our fears for our colleagues are very real. All too often in Iran, the jail terms of foreigners identified as critics of the regime end in death. We know that the lives of the two are hanging by a thread. Green Bundestag member Claudia Roth, who later becomes minister of state for culture, makes a trip to Iran with lawyer and conservative politician Peter Gauweiler, and appeals to the government to release the reporters. German foreign minister Guido Westerwelle also takes up the case. We speak on the phone almost daily. I am moved by how meticulous and passionate he is—the antithesis of a politician in it just for the publicity. We all know that you can't rely on the rule of law in Iran. There, women who have been raped and dare to speak up are stoned to death. Not the male perpetrators. In this kind of country, there is little hope of finding law and justice. It is solely about finding a "face-saving" deal. This is advantageous for Iran, but doesn't mean we throw our principles overboard or allow ourselves to be blackmailed. Fortunately, vanity wins out in the end: A conversation between the German foreign minister and the Iranian president Mahmoud Ahmadinejad is the very acceptable price of a breakthrough. We are relieved, but don't want to celebrate until the two journalists are actually back.

On February 19, 2011, Marcus and Jens are released with fines of $50,000 each. Foreign Minister Guido Westerwelle collects the two reporters in person. After 132 days in jail, they touch down on German soil at five in the morning on February 20—reasonably unscathed.

A few weeks prior to their homecoming, at our company's New

Year reception on January 10, 2011, I devoted my short speech almost exclusively to the case and made a sober appeal to our festive guests:

"For us, an ongoing situation links the old and new years in a sad and symbolic way: For ninety-two days, our colleagues Marcus Hellwig and Jens Koch have been held captive in Tabriz, Iran. Despite urgent public appeals and highly committed behind-the-scenes diplomacy on the part of the German Foreign Ministry, there have been few positive developments. Even a long-awaited Christmas visit from family was postponed several times, and became more of an Iranian media event than part of a solution. There is no prospect of a swift release.

"The lack of a fundamental rule of law and its resulting loss of freedom is terrible. This has become very clear to us—it is concrete, tangible, real. We journalists, both at Axel Springer and elsewhere, talk a lot about political prisoners, censorship, human rights violations, international law, press freedom, and other important issues. But now we ourselves are experiencing—or rather guessing from a distance—what it's really like. Two colleagues who up until recently were happily wandering in and out of our offices, enjoying a sunny espresso at the Ullstein Bar just behind us, have been forced to sit in a windowless cell for ninety-two days. No contact with the outside world, no proper legal representation, and no prospect of a fair trial—let alone release. Please take a moment to imagine what it would be like to spend ninety-two days sitting in a hole with no contact with the outside world—as opposed to standing here sipping champagne. It's important for us to imagine this in detail, because it could have been any of us. A few years ago, a friend of mine, a doctor and well-heeled Berliner, was jailed for just a few days in a Muslim country. He had bought a piece of *stone for 3 euros from a street vendor that was then classified as an antique at the border. This friend still has nightmares, and will always remember what justice feels like in a flawed constitutional state.*

"Of what has the Iranian regime accused our colleagues? A visa violation—because they entered the country as tourists even though they wanted to research a story about Ashtiani being sentenced to death by stoning. In addition to many wonderful messages of solidarity, one or two smart-alecks have contacted us to point out that visa violations are punishable even in the most spotless of democracies. That's true. But here in Germany, journalists can enter the country to carry out whatever research they like. In Iran, the only option was to provide false information—or forgo researching the story altogether. Furthermore: A visa violation in Germany would lead, at worst, to deportation after a few hours. The case of our two reporters makes clear, in a very concrete way, to what extent the rule of law, a reliable rule of law, shapes our quality of life and our seemingly self-evident freedoms. Being made to feel like the plaything of arbitrary power due to an alleged or actual offense remains for me the ultimate lack of freedom. The rule of law is the only answer. Without the rule of law, there is no democracy. Without democracy, no rule of law.

"Compared to other human rights violations in Iran and elsewhere, what our colleagues are going through is relatively benign. But it's still bad enough. So maybe we will see this case as a kind of salutary shock, a shock that could free us from the lethargy and naïveté that mark our current engagement with Islamist fundamentalism. There are many forms of terror and many threats to freedom. But none is so acute—or so virulently endangers our values and our freedoms—as Islamism, the radicalized form of Islam.

The threats are real: Iran's nuclear armament; Hamas suicide attacks; the Stockholm bombings; Berlin's often volatile parallel societies; the fact that homosexuality is officially punishable by death in six Muslim countries; that women who have allegedly had extramarital sex are stoned to death—and, yes, the bitter realization that our reporters have been in jail for ninety-two days simply for wanting to do their jobs."

The words had barely faded away before champagne glasses started clinking again in the wood-paneled rooms of the Journalisten-Club. The good news: Our two reporters have now long since resumed their normal working lives. The bad news: This "salutary shock" has had little effect to date.

WEAKENED FROM WITHIN—
DONALD TRUMP AND
ANGELA MERKEL

It's not only dictators, autocrats, and populists who weaken freedom. Sometimes it's freedom's staunchest allies.

Hardly anyone has weakened democracy from within as much as the 45th president of the United States, Donald Trump. But it would be uninteresting, predictable, and unjust to write about his failings without even briefly illuminating the other side of the coin.

The polarization of American society is certainly not only or even primarily his work. Left-wing politics has contributed its share too, by being increasingly disconnected from the priorities and needs of large parts of the population and full of self-righteousness. Also, if one disregards Trump's narcissistic self-dramatization and an erratic political style that shows little respect for democratic institutions, one sees an administration that made three important course corrections: the economic decoupling from dictatorships, especially China; the growing pressure on Europe to fund and strengthen NATO; and a critical stance against the abusive market-dominating practices of Google, Apple, Amazon, Microsoft, Meta, and, most importantly, Chinese surveillance tools and platforms. These policies have all been continued in Joe Biden's presidency. In style and language, their differences are vast; in substance, strikingly few. Underplaying Trump's leadership on these fronts does no favors to a substantive critique of his democracy-damaging legacy.

From the beginning of his presidential bid, Donald Trump used aggressive and incendiary language, presented simplistic worldviews, and pointedly depicted his opponents as the enemy (US, the good guys, versus THEM, the bad guys). This is the emotional fuel of polarization. His rapid rise was based in part on relativizing racism, and throughout his term, Trump downplayed any cases of police violence against blacks, including the murder of George Floyd in 2020, as isolated incidents. He called protests against racism "un-American."

Deeply associated with Donald Trump's administration are the terms "fake news" and "alternative facts." And it is here that lie the most dangerous, democracy-damaging legacies of his time in office.

Fake news has been around as long as news has been around. For thousands of years, it spread as rumors in the marketplaces and gossip behind closed doors. Today, it spreads globally within seconds on social media. So fake news is not new. It's just become more dangerous. And it becomes a problem for democracy when social groups, political parties, or NGOs accuse the other side of falsifying facts and label facts that do not serve their own agenda as fake. Trump not only reinforced this tendency, he elevated it in his political communications and campaigns.

This phenomenon was compounded at the very beginning of Trump's presidency with the idea of "alternative facts"—perhaps the most dangerous poison to any debate (which is, after all, the basis of democracy) and thus probably one of the most effective underminings of democracy. The occasion was the inauguration of Donald Trump. His press secretary at the time, Sean Spicer, claimed on January 21, 2017, that never before had so many people attended the inauguration of a president. Aerial footage clearly proved otherwise. Asked about this on *Meet the Press*, Trump adviser Kellyanne Conway defended Spicer's statement using the phrase "alternative facts" and spoke of counting methods that would come to a different conclusion. This is a stylistic device of autocracies and dictatorships, which all employ "alternative facts" through targeted disinformation, manipulation, and propaganda. When Putin did not like certain developments, figures, and facts during his invasion of Ukraine, he simply told his citizens the opposite by means of the state-controlled media. Alternative facts convinced the population of the great successes of the Russian army in Ukraine.

But in a democracy, Conway's remarks were like a dam breaking; they were the beginning of a political culture that turns facts into things that can be chosen and asserted at will. It was the destruction of agreed-upon information as the binding basis for knowledge. It was the destruction of reliability and fairness and thus of trust. The negative effects on a democratic society cannot be overestimated. When facts are no longer a reliable foundation, not only does trust fade, but conspiracy theories flourish and finally, because each side has its very own facts, elections become impossible. On what basis should one judge a candidate if everything can be true or false at the same time? One can, and one should, interpret facts differently in a free society, and one can and should argue about whether a fact is really a fact. But at some point, a fact must be accepted by all to be a basis for debate, decision, or compromise. When that does not happen, because facts are treated like opinions, an attitude emerges that is a reversal of the idea of enlightenment. Belief takes precedence over knowledge. It is the end of democracy.

The consequences of alternative facts can be observed in democracies throughout the world today: Polarization of society reinforced by a polarization of the media. Media brands see themselves as amplifiers of a political stance. Some are in the Left camp, others in the Right. Some support this candidate, others that one. In the good old tradition of endorsement shortly before a decisive election, this can be interpreted as a sign of transparency and spurring the formation of political opinion. But when it becomes one-sided, predictable agitation, and thus activism, it is the opposite of journalism.

These developments reinforce the fissuring and insecurity of society. Everyone lives and talks only in a bubble. Each bubble defends its own prejudices. And a democratic community gradually unlearns the wonderful basic virtue of agreeing to disagree. We may have different opinions—some irreconcilable—but we remain in conversation and don't take the disagreement personally. When a society loses this ability, it is headed toward hatred and violence. In America, a direct line is visible from Kellyanne Conway's statement about "alternative facts" to naked violence.

After Joe Biden's narrow victory in November 2020, Donald Trump repeatedly disputed the validity of the election. After several media outlets declared Biden the winner, he said, "The simple fact is this election is far from over" and for weeks referred to the election as a "fraud" and "stolen." As a result, Republican and Democratic partisans were confronting each other in increasingly emotional ways. Instead of coming off as a good citizen, which requires one to acknowledge defeat, Trump and his entourage resorted to increasingly aggressive language. The president's son, Donald Trump Jr., called for "total war" on the election outcome.

The storming of the Capitol on January 6 was the sad and violent climax of this rhetoric. An attack on the heart of American democracy was fueled by the most powerful representative of that democracy itself. That Trump was able to convince so many Americans of his lies about the election and mobilize tens of thousands of them to protest against the certification of the election shows that a significant part of the population is now infected by the virus of alternative facts.

The storming of the Capitol was a coup against democracy, organized from above, by a person who while in office had made key decisions to aid the global guiding power of freedom and the fight against autocrats. It was the end to Donald Trump's presidency and is a warning of what happens when a language of rage and exclusion declares facts to be alternatives, and thus fractures a society. January 6, 2021, will enter the history books as an emblem of how a democracy was attacked not from the outside, but from the inside, by its highest representative, the president himself.

Another, very different example of democracies being weakened from within is Angela Merkel, Germany's former chancellor, who notched up sixteen years in office. During that time, probably no other politician was viewed as a greater symbol of reliability, balance, reason, and moderation. Globally—and especially in the

United States—Merkel was regarded as the epitome of centrist politics, celebrated, and glorified as a beacon and guarantor of democratic leadership. *Time* magazine called her the "Chancellor of the Free World" and named her its 2015 "Person of the Year."

Yet these days, this hero of centrist governance is a symbol of its weaknesses. She misjudged the way of the world, and the performance of her administration is under critical review.

Immigration: Some consider Merkel's actions in the summer of 2015 a humanitarian gesture, others a naïve gamble. The situation in Syria had become more brutal, triggering the worst refugee crisis since the Second World War, according to Frontex. Instead of complying with the Dublin Regulation—stating that the country in which a person is registered first is also the one responsible to process the asylum application—Merkel went solo. Those who made their way to Germany were allowed to stay there. "We can do it" ("*Wir schaffen das*") was her all-encompassing motto, but it turned out to be an empty shell. The combination of overly high numbers of asylum seekers—further amplified by thousands of economic refugees coming from elsewhere—and a completely unprepared administration led to chaos. Instead of defining clear criteria and management processes, she took selfies with arriving refugees. The pictures went viral globally and with them, a message that seemed like an invitation: all refugees welcome. Her move was widely criticized. By going alone on the refugee matter, Merkel divided Germany and Europe. She prompted the rise of the populist party AfD in Germany and turned long-standing friends like Eastern Europe—who had been long admirers of her politics—into foes. Her decision fueled the debate on migration in the UK and was one of the reasons why Brexit supporters prevailed in the 2016 referendum. Until today, Europe and particularly Germany have had to struggle with xenophobia as a reaction to the superficial effort of presenting a tolerant and likable face of Germany. Too much tolerance created intolerance.

Digitization: Germany fell asleep on the job. According to the Digital Economy and Society Index (DESI), in 2022—one year after Merkel left office—Germany sits literally just above the EU average, and Lithuania, Finland, Denmark, the Netherlands, Sweden, Ireland, Malta, Spain, Luxemburg, Estonia, Austria, Slovenia, and France are all doing better. German administrative bodies still work largely in analog mode, with pen and paper. Internet access and cell phone coverage is poor. As the newsmagazine *Der Spiegel* put it: "Germany is a FAX machine." And if Angela Merkel had had her way, the Chinese state-owned company Huawei would have won the contract to expand the German 5G network.

Defense: During the Merkel era, Germany deliberately missed NATO's 2 percent target on a regular basis—contravening the 2006 agreement that all member states would invest a minimum of 2 percent of their GDP in defense. The Federal Statistical Office calculated that a 2 percent expenditure on defense would have required a defense budget of around 71.3 billion euros in 2021, but that year Germany only spent about half that amount. It was Olaf Scholz, Merkel's Social Democrat successor, who rectified this dangerous aberration in December 2021, a few weeks after he took office. It's also worth noting that the United States pays 2.2 times more to defense than all other twenty-eight NATO partners combined—over $800 billion in 2022. Under Angela Merkel, the German military was transformed into an all-volunteer force. The dramatic lack of investments led to the troops' dysfunctional downfall.

THE TRADE TRAP

The transatlantic relationship: In 2017, during a party event in a beer tent at Munich's Trudering festival, Merkel declared, in a veiled allusion to Donald Trump's election as United States president: "The times when we could completely rely on others are pretty much over. . . . We Europeans really need to take our fate into our own hands." Germany should still maintain its friendship with the United States and the UK, of course, but "whenever possible, with Russia and other countries as well." This was a remarkable shift given the decades of strong links with the West. Instead of telling a German public disgusted by Trump that the transatlantic friendship was clearly much deeper and more important than the behavior of a single American president, and would therefore survive his administration, she publicly sought new alliances and partners. And explicitly included Russia. It was as though Angela Merkel had always believed in a special German-Russian path and was now promoting it politically.

Merkel's entire handling of the Nord Stream 2 project seems to bear this out. The 2015 decision to build the pipeline, made shortly after the Russian annexation of Crimea and the invasion of eastern Ukraine, triggered both a security and credibility crisis. Its construction placed extreme strain on United States–German relations and won Germany few European friends. Concerns about the risks of dependency on Russia fell on deaf ears. Even the building of the first Baltic Sea pipeline was controversial. Merkel once called Nord Stream 1 the "largest energy infrastructure project of our time."

Energy: But Merkel's most serious mistake—the basis for much that has followed—was her decision in 2011 to phase out nuclear energy. The catalyst was the Fukushima nuclear accident in Japan on March 11, 2011. As a result of power supply cuts caused by a tsunami, three reactor cores went into meltdown, releasing radioactivity into the atmosphere. Just three days after the disaster and without any evidence of casualties but shortly before a set of state elections, Merkel announced Germany's decisive withdrawal from nuclear energy, with almost no parliamentary debate. Just two and a half months later, the ethics commission she had set up to consider the nuclear phase-out presented its final report, giving the new policy a seal of approval. To this day, there is criticism of the group's lack of scientific independence.

This U-turn was as extreme as it was surprising, because as recently as the fall of the previous year, the conservative-liberal German government had decided to extend the operating life of seventeen German nuclear power plants. Fifty-five years after the first commercial nuclear power plant opened in Europe, the German chancellor decreed the end of the most efficient and climate-friendly energy production in Europe's largest economy—without proper democratic oversight. It looked to some as though the otherwise rational chancellor had let herself be carried away by the emotion of the moment and had opted for a populist solution due to a combination of genuine concerns and superficial opinion polling. Others felt that she had been waiting for a chance to remove the final obstacle to a coalition of the CDU and the Greens, a party that had always categorically rejected nuclear energy. A mere two months after Fukushima, in an ironic punch line, a Green politician became prime minister of a federal state for the first time—in Baden-Württemberg of all places, which had almost seen fifty-eight years of continuous conservative CDU rule.

One thing is for sure: Angela Merkel, building on the negligent decisions of her predecessors—especially Putin's friend and former Rosneft Oil executive Gerhard Schröder—contributed in no small part to Germany's dependence on Russian gas. Putin controls both the gas tap and German fortunes. And he is not afraid to use blackmail. Gas supplies via Nord Stream 1 were halted several times in 2022—mostly for completely spurious reasons, such as supposedly defective turbines or oil leaks—and later entirely stopped as a result of the pipeline explosions in fall of that year. Energy prices rose sharply. Inflation in Germany climbed to over 10 percent, and it rose even higher in most other European countries. Given all this, it is hardly surprising that energy dependency has increasingly morphed into economic dependency. Life is more expensive for everyone, and those already on low incomes face a terrifying struggle to survive. As a result, the German government has been forced to provide support packages worth billions of euros. This is the price of an economic dependency that was allowed to grow unchecked for years.

While Germany imported goods worth 16.3 billion euros from Russia in 2004, this figure rose to 33.1 billion euros in 2021. That's more than double. Exports to Russia rose from 15 billion euros to 26.6 billion euros in the same period. German direct investment in Russia rose from 15.8 billion euros in 2010 to over 25.5 billion euros in 2019. Style-wise, Angela Merkel had established a new form of politics. One that was transactional, unideological, pragmatic, and—in sharp contrast to most of her male peers—stunningly lacking vanity.

The bottom line is nevertheless poor: After sixteen years

in office, Angela Merkel weakened Germany, Europe, and the transatlantic alliance while strengthening an authoritarian Russia—with which the West now has to deal.

Was that naïveté, opportunism, or strategy? Since Angela Merkel certainly isn't naïve, let's hope it has been opportunism.

"A Good Day for Russia"

On May 30, 2011, I'm sitting with some of our editors up on the roof of the Russian Embassy on Unter den Linden in Berlin. It's a balmy day, and the ambassador has invited us to dine with him. Earlier that day, Chancellor Angela Merkel held a press conference announcing Germany's plan to shut down its nuclear power plants.

The ambassador looks over at the Reichstag from the belvedere of the late Stalinist-era building and, as the dinner starts, raises a full vodka glass, which matches those standing before us. In a friendly voice he says: "To the health of the German government! This is a good day for Russian energy policy, this is a good day for Russia. Nastrovje!" Somewhat embarrassed, we all raise our glasses. Exactly one month later, on June 30, 2011, the German Bundestag passes the plan to phase out nuclear energy, with 513 out of 600 members voting in favor.

It wasn't to our health the Russian ambassador was drinking.

PART III

THE ESCALATION: THE CHINA CHALLENGE

On a Plane with Helmut Kohl—
My First Encounter with "Wandel
durch Handel"

*In 1995, for the first time in my life, I'm on the "chancellor's plane,"
the German version of Air Force One. I'm the youngest journalist
on board, and by far the least important. Correspondents and reporters from all the major German and international media outlets are grouped at the back of the Airbus A310, named "Theodor
Heuss" after a former German president. The business delegation
is in the middle section. It contains the crème de la crème of the
German economy: CEOs from a number of top companies, including Gerhard Cromme (Krupp), Heinrich von Pierer (Siemens),
Rolf-Dieter Leister (Deutsche Telekom), Jürgen Weber (Lufthansa),
Henning Schulte-Noelle (Allianz), and Mark Wössner (Bertels-
mann). Also on board is Lars Windhorst—Kohl's "Wunderkind," a
mere nineteen years of age. He founded his first company two years
previously with a Chinese businessman, importing electronics and
computer parts from Asia.*

*Later it is said that no other state visit by a chancellor ever
involved so many high-level business representatives. But this is*

no ordinary state visit. The aim of the trip—lasting from November 12 to 21, and including stops in Vietnam and Singapore—is to lay the foundations for a completely new kind of Sino-German economic relationship. Toward the front of the plane are the chancellery staff, and at the very front, right by the cockpit, is the chancellor's suite. Here sits Helmut Kohl, the "Chancellor of German Reunification," who has led Germany for thirteen years already. Every now and then, he wanders down to the back of the plane, answers questions from journalists and business leaders, and cracks a few jokes. A dark blue cardigan is draped over his mountainous belly.

After a few hours, Kohl's spokesperson comes to me and says curtly: The chancellor wants to see you. My heart sinks into my boots. I follow him to the front and suddenly I'm alone with Helmut Kohl. He asks me a few questions, and wants to know who this young journalist is that someone recommended for the trip. Then he drinks a tomato juice spritzer and holds forth. He tells me that the German economy has missed opportunities in China (our esteemed CEOs need to get up a bit earlier). That a new chapter has now begun. That this trip alone will generate Chinese orders to the tune of several billion Deutsche Mark for Germany. That the only way we can secure prosperity at home is via access to these huge markets. At some point, in a shaky voice, I dare to ask his view on human rights violations in China. Kohl waves a hand, somewhat irritated by the question. Of course, he says, not everything is the same there as it is at home. But given the history of the Great Thousand-Year Empire, this isn't something we should expect. The best way to improve conditions in China is through trade—"Wandel durch Handel." I think this was the very first time I heard the phrase.

We're received with military honors in Beijing. In the course of the visit, talks are held between Kohl and Chinese premier Li Peng. There's a one-on-one meeting with President Jiang Zemin (Kohl gifts him two flutes), a state banquet (Kohl requests the AC be turned down), and visits to showcase companies. Contracts are signed and business leaders announce strategic deals. Human rights issues are only discreetly raised. No one knows whether this is done with serious intent or just to pacify the left-wing media back home. There are evening briefings for the journalists, where a witty Kohl holds court and tells jokes. There is a press conference in which the German chancellor summarizes the visit and its key outcomes in satisfied, optimistic tones. He wraps it up as follows: This country [China] will increasingly open up to international development in the coming years. I feel it is extremely important that we Germans support this. It is thus vital that as many young Germans as possible find their way here, so they can get to know the people, the culture, and the mindset of this great and fascinating land. I think we are on the right track.

The days are characterized by hustle and bustle, along with a certain degree of pomposity. Above it all, waving like a flag, is the reassuring phrase that smothers any lingering doubts: "change through trade." Everything will be fine.

On the evening of our final day in Beijing, the entire delegation heads to a Chinese restaurant. The chancellor would like something "traditional." And this is exactly what he gets. The menu includes honey-glazed grasshoppers and whole frogs grilled on bamboo stems. Waiters come to the tables and slit open live snakes so that their blood can be dripped into shot glasses of liqueur. The guests begin to turn pale and start making dumb jokes. A banquet that's a test of courage. Dog is also available on request, and this particularly amuses our table of journalists. For Kohl certainly couldn't be toppled in the normal scheme of things. He's the "eternal chancellor." But if Germans were to see photos of him eating dog alongside a photo of a cute Chinese puppy, then he'd be gone. The evening dissolves into wine-fueled merriment. Kohl doesn't eat any dog. He has the sweet-and-sour pork instead.

DEPENDENCE ON CHINA

China's thinking is ambitious and long-term. Ambitious, because a country with over 1.4 billion people and a GDP of over $17.7 trillion in 2021 has to think big. And long-term because China can afford to think long-term. China has a 3,500-year history and a non-democratic form of governance, on which mid-term priorities like election cycles and even media trends have no disruptive effects.

China at the beginning of the twenty-first century thinks and acts like a monarchy. It is a communist kingdom. And a nationalistic cadre-monarchy of high-speed totalitarian capitalism. Over the past three decades, China has created a model that appears to be supremely successful: a totalitarian state economy combining the advantages of a democratic market economy with the rigorous discipline of a totalitarian regime, which has created faster growth and prosperity than any other model in the world. But if China is to be our new economic role model, then the West will have to throw its values overboard—especially freedom of expression, the rule of law, and human rights. And any realistic climate targets. If that's not what we want, we have to end our economic and growing political dependence on China.

Here's what's remarkable: China somehow managed to be viewed as a virtually normal democratic market economy all around the globe. At the World Economic Forum in Davos in 2017, China's head of state and secretary general of the Chinese Communist Party (CCP), Xi Jinping, who likes to be called president, sounded to many like the voice of economic reason. "Pursuing protectionism is like locking oneself in a dark room. While wind and rain may be kept outside, so are light and air," he said in his speech. Members of his own delegation, who were in the audience, laughed as he explained the importance of the free flow of ideas, people, and capital—all of which are highly restricted in modern China. But the largely European audience lapped it up. Donald Trump, on the other hand, looked like a populist poltergeist during the 2016 presidential election—and confirmed this impression at his inauguration ("America First!"). I'm willing to bet that if European business leaders had been asked at that point which one they'd rather be ruled by, a majority would have chosen Xi.

Here's what gets forgotten: China has been ruled with an iron fist for seven decades by the CCP, which today numbers close to one hundred million members. Tens of millions died in the famine caused by Mao Zedong's "Great Leap Forward," and in the labor camps where citizens were imprisoned for "thought crimes" during the madness of the "Great Proletarian Cultural Revolution." And aging autocrats turned People's Liberation Army guns on demonstrators in Tiananmen Square in 1989. This homogeneous, centralized state is still a one-party state, and is becoming increasingly totalitarian under Xi. The country's economic shift at the end of the 1970s to a form of controlled capitalism (or "socialist market economy," as Beijing has termed it since 1992) hasn't altered the fact that the Party carries out "central economic planning" each year. Efforts to control and influence both the public and private sector are plentiful. CCP representatives are to sit on the corporate boards of every state-owned enterprise. Listed companies are required to establish internal party units since 2018. There are residents' committees in every neighborhood. And right now millions of Uyghurs are being held in "re-education camps" simply because of their ethnicity and religion. China is and remains a ruthlessly controlled dictatorship in the guise of a modern economic power.

And this regime has ambitious goals. The plans of the Chinese elites and especially party leader Xi Jinping are clearly formulated. By 2049, China wants to be the leading global economic power, but beyond that, it also wants to bring about "material, political, cultural and ethical, social, and ecological advancement." This is what Xi announced in his 2017 CCP National Congress speech, and he strengthened it five years later in the same context. Behind this seemingly innocuous formulation lies an elaborate plan that is carefully scheduled to coincide with a key historical milestone: 2049 will mark the one hundredth anniversary of the People's Republic of China, founded by Mao. The overall goal is a communist unitary state that creates a "superior" people and nation. It is a vision based on millennia of claims to power—in party parlance, the goal is the "rejuvenation of the Chinese nation." The aim is to put China back where it belongs, according to its own world-historical perspective. At the top. Number one.

However, this goal of total dominance can only be achieved through the creation of economic dependencies and political influence around the world. Countries dependent on China will eventually have to accept Chinese rules. This means: Surveillance systems and restrictions on free speech will make their way into democracies. Those refusing to fall into line will quickly and decisively be discarded. America and Europe could well end up as second-class world powers—mere economic service providers.

Some argue: China may be more than just an economic power, but it's far too smart to launch military offensives. An illustration of just how naïve this position is comes courtesy of Nancy Pelosi's trip to Taiwan in summer 2022. Following the announcement that the speaker of the United States House of Representatives was planning to visit, China reacted with firm opposition and threats. The United States would be subjected to "serious consequences" if the Democrat actually traveled to Taiwan, said a Foreign Ministry spokesperson in Beijing. When Pelosi went ahead anyway and touched down in Taiwan on August 2, 2022, China immediately took punitive action. The United States ambassador to Beijing was summoned; climate talks with the United States were halted; sanctions were imposed on Pelosi herself; further threats and countermeasures followed. But most significantly, China launched one of the largest military maneuvers since the 1995 missile crisis. Right after Pelosi's arrival, the military began a four-day training exercise. Twenty-one Chinese Air Force warplanes took off in the direction of Taiwan. Live-fire drills were conducted in six areas near the coast. Air and sea traffic had to be halted, which essentially amounted to a blockade.

It is simply incorrect that China is too pragmatic to launch military offensives. For decades, the facts have told a different story. China wants to build the world's largest armed forces, and is investing huge sums to that end. The scale of the Chinese military is already mind-boggling. According to *Global Firepower*—which has been publishing a yearly military strength ranking since 2005—China has two million armed soldiers and another half a million in reserve—that's 37 percent more than the U.S. It also has almost 180,000 tanks and armored vehicles, 3,300 aircraft and helicopters, as well as more than 730 ships and more than 400 nuclear weapons. And spending on the military is soaring. According to the Stockholm International Peace Research Institute, China has upped its military budget almost sixfold since 2006, to $293.4 billion in 2021. By comparison, United States spending, while totaling over $800 billion, has increased only by 43.4 percent over the same period of time.

However, China's military ambitions go far beyond official defense budgets. In recent years, Xi Jinping and his regime have repeatedly called for a "civil-military fusion"—a militarization of all sections of society and a blurring of the lines between civic and military institutions. This strategy or policy is intended to turn the People's Liberation Army into a supreme military body.

China is also planning to claim global leadership in other areas by 2049. It sees research as a strategic tool and promotes and drives it as intensively as possible. A key factor in achieving Chinese global dominance is artificial intelligence (AI), which is rapidly becoming the premier instrument of power. Whoever dominates AI's innovation, development, and use will dominate the world. That's why the new arms race is no longer just a conventional battle between East and West, but an increasingly technological one between China and America. Europe has lagged behind in this field and no longer plays a significant role. And while Silicon Valley was once clearly the AI superpower, China is now quickly catching up.

In 2020, for the first time, citations from Chinese scientific journal articles on AI topped those from the United States. The sheer wealth of data the country generates is accelerating that trend. By 2030, an estimated five billion consumer devices in China will be connected via the Internet of Things. And where global technological superiority is not yet given, surveillance and prohibition still do the trick.

China has banned ChatGPT from the very beginning and is pushing Baidu's home-made bot Ernie instead—which was "far from perfect" at launch, to put it in its CEO's own words. This local rival of ChatGPT is in line with China's strict censorship. When asked a critical question about the regime or any disgraced individual, the bot merely suggests starting a new conversation. China has a deep understanding of the power of AI answer machines. By controlling the bias of the algorithms, it aims to control its people's mindset. Competition or diversity is unwelcome.

China is a champion of double standards and preferential treatment for its own products on an international level. TikTok's congressional hearing in March 2023 was only one example. If the U.S. were to force a sale of TikTok based on serious data and privacy concerns, it would face firm opposition from China. According to the Chinese Ministry of Commerce, "Forcing the sale of TikTok will seriously damage the confidence of investors from all over the world, including from China, on investing in the United States." A statement that proves what has long been denied: TikTok is a tool in the very interest and under the influence of the CCP.

AI is often capable of more than is ethically desirable or acceptable. That's why democratic countries, particularly the United States, are developing regulatory boundaries. Just because something is technically possible doesn't mean that it should be allowed:

In areas involving surveillance and manipulation, regulations and laws curb AI excesses that would violate human dignity. Not so in a dictatorship like China. Anything that serves the interests of the Chinese unitary state and the CCP is permitted. The combination of a disproportionately large data haul from a 1.4-billion-strong population and an unethical regulatory framework creates advantages in terms of developmental speed and quality. China has either already achieved global dominance or it will achieve it in a few years' time. The question then is how the West will react. In what kind of global system will AI prosper? Unilateral or bilateral? Diverse and competitive or homogeneous and monopolistic? In one that is rules-based or where "might is right"? The answers to these questions are critical for our world order and democracy's survival.

But AI is only one of the two key fields where the bilateral arms race of the future will play out. The second is biotechnology and genetic engineering. State capitalism offers advantages here too. Chinese doctors are already manipulating children's genetic material. They are using CRISPR/Cas9 techniques to alter DNA, for example to protect children from being infected with HIV. From China's point of view, it seems both feasible and desirable to "optimize" children before birth. CRISPR and gene manipulation may be used not simply to prevent diseases, but to create perfectly designed human beings. Selecting a child's gender, hair color, eye color, height, and even a higher IQ now seem within reach. Biotech could end up becoming a valuable tool in the global power struggle. CRISPR techniques might be weaponized to create a "superior" people.

Likely the largest "research project" in this area has been running since the end of 2017. Police in China are collecting blood samples from millions of men and boys in order to build a genetic database, according to a *New York Times* report published in 2020. This is an attempt to harness genetics as a means of monitoring the population. Samples from just 5 to 10 percent of the entire male population are enough for comprehensive analysis: Genetic identification of relatives means that a system covering the entire population can be built with just a small number of individuals. These blood samples are being collected systematically, and according to a study from the Australian Strategic Policy Institute, this even involves visits to schools. DNA collection isn't new in China. The DNA of certain groups has been repeatedly scrutinized. In Tibet, the police are already said to hold the DNA of 25 to 33 percent of the population. The creation of a nationwide database takes all of this to new heights. There is a simple statistical reason why men's DNA is being collected: Men commit more crimes than women. In addition to fighting crime—which casts a shadow of suspicion over entire social groups—the DNA database opens the door to social manipulation and control. Findings from the DNA analysis about diseases or disabilities, for example, could be used to the detriment of those affected.

True to Xi Jinping's directive—that the CCP must run all aspects of life in China—everything is meticulously planned and monitored by the CCP. That includes education, the media, and online censorship. In 2013, more than two million people alone were tasked with policing the Internet. In 2021, it was reported that China's Internet police was "stretched to the limit," and that authorities were considering resorting to the use of bots and AI. In August 2022, for instance, keylogging capabilities recording every keystroke on a smartphone were found in TikTok. Experts also found one such program—alongside other mass data collection features—embedded in the CCP app *Xuexi Qiangguo* ("Study and Strengthen the Nation"), which all party members and public administration employees are obliged to use. Video surveillance in cities has been perfected with advanced facial recognition and motion detectors. This surveillance even goes beyond territorial borders. China has reportedly established overseas police service stations, particularly in Europe, through which it is "convincing" dissidents to return to China.

Meanwhile, reproduction is subject to ever-changing central government policy. For decades, the goal was to reduce the birth rate. The one-child policy was implemented with an iron fist—anyone with more than a single child faced heavy fines. Few exceptions were granted, including to ethnic minorities. As a result, infanticide was not uncommon. In 2016, the one-child policy was abolished, allowing parents to have two children as population growth was freshly viewed as desirable. In 2021, restrictions were further loosened to a three-child limit and then entirely removed.

Xi has been general secretary of the CCP since 2012 and head of state since March 14, 2013. The Party now sees the beginning of the Xi era as marking the end of Deng Xiaoping's period of reforms and opening up. However, this was long ignored or misunderstood by the West as a further opening up or even democratization of China. In fact, Xi has remade the country according to his own ideas and continues to expand his powers. While the CCP's powers are rooted in the constitution, the latter has no great significance in China. Xi has abandoned consensus rule at the top of the Party, rejects any separation of powers, and has abolished the two-term limit on the so-called presidency. He could thus remain in power for life. Many already speak of a personality cult like Mao's. His untrammeled power is also cementing feudal conditions in the Communist People's Republic.

Xi is "modernizing" the country—as a unique, technologically perfected surveillance state. And yes, "*Wandel durch Handel*" may be happening under Xi. But it is change that will lead to an even more totalitarian Chinese state. Xi's personal vision, the "Great Rejuvenation" of China, has a very strong racial element. Implicitly—and sometimes also explicitly—the Great Rejuvenation refers to the expansion of the Han Chinese ethnic group, which forms over 90 percent of the Chinese population. All of which is to the detriment of (Chinese) ethnic minorities.

Xi's reconfiguration of China can be seen in a number of areas. Already in the 1990s, following the Tiananmen Square massacre, "patriotic education" had been introduced for children at elementary schools and beyond. Since September 2021, there have been special textbooks containing Xi Jinping's ideas. Under the guise of protecting minors, anything deemed too Western has been banned. In the mid-2010s, memes of Xi Jinping and the children's book character Winnie the Pooh were widely circulated on the Internet—many had noticed a certain similarity between the two. As a result, any use of A. A. Milne's bear in connection with Xi was banned. Video tutoring classes from abroad, as well as private, on-site Chinese tutoring sessions, are now generally prohibited because their content is harder for the state to control. Minors are now only allowed to play online video games with ID for three hours a week, from 8 p.m. to 9 p.m. on Fridays, Saturdays, and Sundays. An editorial in a government newspaper called video games "spiritual opium."

There's been a shift in economic policy as well. After years of

Chinese tech companies basking in the Chinese leadership's favor, the signals are now very different. The IPO of payment service Ant, an Alibaba subsidiary, was canceled at short notice because the CCP was perturbed by statements from Alibaba CEO Jack Ma. Since then, Ma has virtually disappeared from the public eye for more than two years.

Fear and intimidation are the CCP's most important tools when it comes to consolidating its regime.

The case of writer and activist Liu Xiaobo made global headlines. The former president of the Independent Chinese PEN Center was arrested in December 2008 for "inciting subversion of state power" and later sentenced to eleven years in prison. On Human Rights Day, together with around three hundred other intellectuals, he had published "Charter 08," calling for more democracy in China. In 2010, he was awarded the Nobel Peace Prize in absentia—his chair left symbolically empty. The list of countries that boycotted the award ceremony speaks for itself: Afghanistan, Egypt, China, Iraq, Iran, Kazakhstan, Colombia, Cuba, Morocco, Pakistan, the Philippines, Russia, Saudi Arabia, Serbia, Sudan, Tunisia, Ukraine (whose president at the time was Putin's friend Viktor Fedorovych Yanukovych), Venezuela, and Vietnam. Norway, the country where the ceremony took place, subsequently felt the full wrath of Beijing. Diplomatic relations were put on ice for six years. In 2017, Liu died of liver cancer in a Chinese hospital. He had been denied treatment abroad. His funeral was controversial too: His ashes were scattered at sea to avoid creating any kind of memorial. Even the dead are controlled in China. I once asked a Chinese acquaintance why China acts so ruthlessly in these kinds of cases, without any thought for public perceptions. Her answer was revealing: "Because we can."

The Chinese "legal system" is merciless. Offenses are severely punished. No other country imposes and carries out the death penalty as frequently as China. In 2021, according to Amnesty International, Iran executed at least 314 people, Egypt at least 83 people, and the United States 11 people (bad enough). In China, however, Amnesty estimates that several thousand people are executed every year. The exact figures are not available because the regime keeps them under wraps. Investigating and reporting on them could be dangerous.

The death penalty for people with opposing views is the most extreme form of intimidation in China. But people's behavior is also controlled through maximum levels of surveillance. For several years, a so-called social credit system has been tested in a growing number of cities. Citizens—but also companies and organizations—are evaluated using a points system. Points are added for "correct" behavior and deducted for "incorrect" behavior. Those with poor scores find it more difficult to get loans or insurance, and have a tough time finding a flat or building a career. Those with good scores have easier access to visas or cheaper airline tickets. People who are disadvantaged by the system obviously tend not to speak out. However, Chinese people are often heard saying that they have no problem with "social scoring"— because if you have nothing to hide, you have nothing to fear. And those who behave well are rewarded. Young people in particular have quickly become used to the system. One reason for this is that its mechanisms of punishment and reward are deliberately lifted from the world of computer games. An especially telling argument in support of scoring is the following: In the China of the past, some found themselves denounced and punished purely due to the accusations of a third party. Such incidents were completely unpredictable, subjective, and arbitrary. Today at least, everything is monitored, recorded, and thus, in a manner of speaking, objectively documented. This has made dealing with the Communist Party and the state more predictable. Surveillance as a guarantor of greater justice. The "social credit system" has not yet been rolled out nationwide, partly because face masks have made facial recognition difficult. But it is being implemented more and more widely.

Control over the population is also systematically carried out through audio and video surveillance. Voice, face, and movement profiles are linked to online behavior and other data. Of an estimated one billion cameras worldwide, more than half are in China. Of the twelve cities with the most cameras per capita in the world in 2021, nine are in China.

The WeChat app is another key tool for exerting control. The Chinese can use the app to chat and make phone calls, but also to pay for things. They can order food from every conceivable store; have their favorite meal delivered from every possible restaurant in the city; order cabs; look for jobs; share their location; apply for medical appointments and visas. The app is linked to people's ID cards, and virtually nothing in China works without it. And the state seems to read everything. According to several media outlets, it is not uncommon for users to have their WeChat account blocked if, for example, they call the "wrong" person or send a private message that is deemed inflammatory or suspicious by state observers or software. If that happens, the app has to be unblocked by the user at great expense. A digital censorship made in China.

A well-known Chinese pop star once told me that every fan message he receives or responds to is monitored, every line of his song lyrics is censored.

In the wake of COVID-19, a so-called "Health Code" app has also been rolled out via WeChat, which gives a glimpse into how control can be exerted in the name of fighting a pandemic. Only those who had a green code—and could thus "prove" that they neither have COVID-19 nor have come into contact with an infected person—were able to move about freely. At the entrances to apartment blocks, public buildings, supermarkets, and shopping centers, people had to check in via a QR code and show their color code: If it was orange or red rather than green, they were denied entry and required to report to the local health authority. Following evaluation, they would either be admitted to an isolation hospital or have to quarantine at home. However, a case in Henan Province has shown how a person's health status can be instrumentalized for political purposes. In June 2022, when a group took a train to attend a protest in the provincial capital Zhengzou, their health status turned red just as they reached their destination. They were sent straight back home and missed the protest. Some call the "Health Code" app a modern shackle.

On a far larger scale, this kind of state surveillance also applies to the Uyghurs. In 2022, extensive research by an international consortium of fourteen media outlets documented the oppression of China's Muslim minority. Nearly eleven million Uyghurs live in China. By comparison, the Han Chinese, the largest and most dominant ethnic group, number around 1.2 billion people. They have their own "fast lane" at checkpoints and are given favorable treatment in many areas of life. The Chinese government also settles Han Chinese in regions where it wants to alter the composition of the resident population. Conversely, and in the spirit of a homogeneous unitary state, the CCP regards Muslims with suspicion. For many years it has held them in "re-education camps" so large that they are visible as color spots from space. Millions of Uyghurs are arbitrarily detained in inhumane conditions, subjected to intensive brainwashing, and thanks to an ultra-modern security apparatus, permanently controlled and monitored in their everyday lives. In 2020, evidence surfaced of Huawei's involvement in testing facial recognition software designed to detect Uyghur faces. If a Uyghur was identified during checks, a "Uyghur alert" would automatically be triggered, meaning that the authorities could theoretically be informed of their location. Huawei denies commercial use of the technology, but admits to testing it.

Surveillance and control of Uyghurs intrudes on even the most intimate and private of spheres: Uyghur women have reportedly been forced to have abortions or contraceptive IUDs fitted. So far, UN representatives have not been allowed access to the camps. A number of countries have now accused China of genocide. China no longer denies the existence of the camps, but calls them "Vocational and Education Training Centers."

The Uyghurs are not an isolated case. Tibetans fell victim to Chinese cultural annihilation when China marched into the Himalayan country more than seventy years ago. Even today, any meeting between a politician and the Dalai Lama is viewed as a provocation in China—and has diplomatic consequences.

In Tibet, the process of repression is complete. In Hong Kong, it is still in full swing. When Britain agreed to hand over the colony on July 1, 1997, China assured Hong Kong that it would retain extensive autonomy for fifty years. The CCP mainly agreed to this deal because Hong Kong was China's most important trading port in the 1990s. However, China's admission to the WTO in 2001 and its construction of new home ports significantly lowered its dependence on Hong Kong. China began to increase pressure on the "Special Administrative Region," leading to protests.

First came the 2014 "Umbrella Movement," which called for free elections, then the 2019 protests against a proposed bill allowing the extradition of prisoners, or indeed anyone wanted by the CCP, to the mainland. The face of the protests was Joshua Wong, a human rights activist since the age of fourteen in 2011, who has been repeatedly jailed by the authorities. During a visit to the German capital, he described Hong Kong as the new Berlin in a new Cold War. That he allowed himself to be photographed with German politicians at an Axel Springer event, including Foreign Minister Heiko Maas, displeased Beijing greatly. When we spoke on the roof terrace of the Bundestag—the building of the German parliament—on the final evening of his visit, I asked him why he was returning to Hong Kong. His answer: Because I can't abandon all those who are fighting for freedom. I doubled down: But you know that could mean prison or risking your life? Yes, I know, he said. A year later, we heard that Wong had been jailed. The official reason: "Participation in an unauthorized assembly."

In 2020, China passed a controversial National Security Law that many view as a breach of the 1984 Declaration—as only the Hong Kong government technically has the power to pass such a law. It stipulates heavy prison sentences for offenses such as "terrorist activities" and "cooperating with foreign powers to endanger national security." The law is so vague and punitive that it prohibits virtually any form of criticism or dissent, not only in the territory itself but worldwide, as it calls for universal jurisdiction. Hong Kong's case shows that the CCP adheres to treaties only as long as it benefits from them.

Several years later, in May 2023, when Axel Springer exhibited a replica of Jens Galshiøt's *Pillar of Shame* sculpture pointing out Beijing's human rights abuses in Tibet, Xinjiang, Hong Kong, and Taiwan, the Chinese Embassy was quick to react and condemn this move on its website. "The issues of Hong Kong, Xinjiang, and Tibet are purely internal Chinese affairs. Our country therefore strongly opposes any interference by external forces under the guise of human rights into China's internal matters and legal sovereignty." And furthermore: "The Taiwan issue is not about democracy. Taiwan has always been an inseparable part of China's territory." The message is clear: Don't mess with our business.

Yet Taiwan is the most acute and dangerous case. Here too the West has bowed to growing pressure from China over the years. Known officially as the Republic of China, Taiwan has always fought for its independence. But instead of maintaining at least equally cordial diplomatic relations with both countries, Taiwan is treated by most like an illegitimate movement. In Germany, like in the U.S., there is no ambassador but only a representative. The extremely well-read, former German literature student and smart policy broker Professor Dr. Jhy-Wey Shieh is treated as persona non grata. Nobody in the business community and very, very few people in political circles want to be seen or—worse—be photographed with him. Back in October 2022, I attended the national holiday reception of the Taipei Representation Office in Germany. The only person I knew was a correspondent from an Axel Springer publication. I checked the guest list: not a single relevant government representative, not a single business leader of importance. It was the most avoided event of the year in the German capital.

The People's Republic of China sees itself as the only legitimate government of Chinese territory. And its aim is the "peaceful reunification" of all territories—including Taiwan, even though the archipelago, unlike Hong Kong or Macau, has never been under Communist rule. This "reunification"—a psychologically astute euphemism—will be fought for "to the end" and "at any cost," according to Beijing defense minister Wei Fenghe at the Shangri-La security conference on June 12, 2022. His speech was covered in detail by the world's leading media. The choice of words was remarkable—especially given Putin's war on Ukraine—and must have surprised many who wish to see China as a peaceful, pragmatic visionary for economic growth. "Those who pursue Taiwanese independence in an attempt to split China will definitely come to no good end. No one should ever underestimate the resolve and ability of the Chinese armed forces to safeguard its territorial integrity."

As part of its nationwide mobility and highway expansion plans, China has repeatedly formulated the intention of connecting Taiwan to the mainland—an unpopular concept in Taiwan that did not involve its consent or contribution. The plans became more concrete in recent years with the presentation of the National Highway Network Plan in 2022, which aims to complete all network enlargements by 2035. This tunnel or bridge might just be the due date for China's "reunification" ambitions. If Taiwan remains independent after 2035, the Chinese government would lose face. Hence the annexation may happen much earlier.

Taiwan is a symbolic test case for the current world order. If

Taiwan falls because the West failed to act, then our submission will begin to be irrevocable.

China makes no secret of its ambitions for Taiwan. For example, in its 2022 White Paper, a sort of strategy document, the CCP—referring to itself as Communist Party of China (CPC)—writes: "Under the strong leadership of the CPC Central Committee with Xi Jinping at the core, the CPC and the Chinese government have adopted new and innovative measures in relation to Taiwan." As a result, "the wheel of history rolls on toward national reunification, and it will not be stopped by any individual or any force." The government of Taiwan (freely elected, unlike the CCP) must be removed. And the threats become quite specific. Reunification by peaceful means is the "first choice" of the Chinese government, "but we will not renounce the use of force, and we reserve the option of taking all necessary measures."

China remains Taiwan's largest trading partner. In 2020, Taiwanese exports to China totaled $102.45 billion, twice as much as to the United States. Taiwan also plays a significant role for the rest of the world. As the largest manufacturer of semiconductors, Taiwanese businesses generate over 65 percent of global sales in this area and control 90 percent of the most advanced and sophisticated production of microprocessors. This product is indispensable in a number of industries: electronic devices, cars, and not least, weapons. A sudden annexation of Taiwan would lead either to a heightened level of Western dependence on China—or the collapse of a range of industries. The following example shows why.

In 2021, the factories of major car companies such as Volkswagen, Opel, BMW, General Motors, and Daimler came to a standstill all around the world, because China couldn't meet their demand for microchips. The automotive industry lost approximately $240 billion in sales as a result. This is a small illustration of what would happen if Taiwan were annexed by China in the near future. The country's importance in the global microchip and semiconductor market has become an added incentive for Beijing to take over Taiwan. China is already one of the major leaders in extracting and processing rare earths, like lithium or cobalt, used in the developments of batteries, smartphones, and more. In fact, Europe imports 98 percent of its rare earth needs from China. In the long term, America and Europe might be able to break free of this dependence, but not in the short term. Once more, China has leverage that could weaken, if not largely paralyze, the American and European economies overnight. The political implications are obvious. The United States will think twice before mounting a military defense of Taiwan's independence, lest it put Silicon Valley at risk.

The West's dependence on China continues to rise even without the special risk posed by Taiwan. This is particularly so in the European Union's largest economy: Germany. In 2020, around 7 percent of German direct investment was spent in China. It roughly doubled in the previous decade. And China isn't just a highly attractive sales market for Germany. As an "extended workbench" with low wages, China makes the products we use daily—and thus life in and of itself—more affordable. In 2020, *WELT* carried out research on various products manufactured in China, and calculated how much the same goods would cost in Germany if they were produced there in the same way. The results were shocking. For example, if a child's stuffed toy were manufactured exclusively in Germany—with local raw materials and labor—it would cost around 35 euros instead of 12 euros.

Outsourcing production to China—with working conditions that would breach all European legal and ethical standards—has led customers to expect low prices that are divorced from genuine costs. While ever-higher employee standards are enforced in Germany, more and more work is being shifted over to China, where the cheapest possible production can be found in frequently inhumane conditions, with starvation wages and child labor.

For a long time, a so-called joint venture constraint applied in China: If a foreign company wanted to produce things in China, it could only do so with a Chinese partner. This meant that big profits remained in China, and that there was significant technology transfer. At the end of the 2010s, these rules were relaxed, probably because China now has strong players in the auto industry itself.

Despite these rules, China was and still is the most important market for the German automotive industry. In 2022, the VW group sold close to 40 percent of its cars in China, its competitors Daimler and BMW around 33 percent each—with an overall long-term upward trend. This key German industry generates almost eight hundred thousand jobs and a large portion of total European direct investment in China. According to a *Rhodium Group* study, BMW, VW, Daimler, and BASF were collectively responsible for a third of European monetary flow between 2018 and 2021.

Conversely, Chinese automakers are increasingly trying to gain a foothold in Europe via acquisitions and investments—or even partnerships, as the example of the German car rental company Sixt and the Chinese car manufacturer BYD shows. In October 2022, Sixt committed to buy around one hundred thousand e-cars from Chinese car manufacturer BYD by 2028, in order to meet its aim of electrifying 70 to 90 percent of its domestic fleet by

2030. So a German company decides to buy a hundred thousand cars from a company that is subsidized by a totalitarian Communist regime. Whether that is a coincidence or rather the CCP's strategy to weaken the German car industry after enough know-how has been transferred to China is an interesting discussion. One in which no German mobility CEO dares to participate—because they are all already financially dependent on China.

In 2022, Mercedes-Benz, a subsidiary of Daimler, sold around 788,000 out of a total of 2.45 million cars and vans in China. Two Chinese companies now hold a combined stake of nearly 20 percent in the Stuttgart-based auto manufacturer. This has led to close ties between the German company and China, with any disruption to that relationship having serious consequences for business.

The experiences of former Daimler CEO Dieter Zetsche are another resonant and symbolic warning. On Monday, February 5, 2018, Mercedes's PR department posted an Instagram photo of a white Mercedes with an innocuous quote from the Dalai Lama: "Look at situations from all angles, and you will become more open." Given that the Dalai Lama—probably the world's most peace-loving person—is China's public enemy number one, this was viewed as an affront. A wave of outrage swept across the Internet. On Tuesday, Mercedes deleted the photo and posted an apology on the Chinese microblogging site *Weibo*: It was aware that it had "deeply hurt the feelings of the Chinese people." However, this did not seem to placate the Chinese government. On Wednesday, a Beijing newspaper described Daimler as an "enemy of the people." In response, Mercedes made an even bigger apology: Company boss Zetsche wrote a letter to Shi Mingde, the Chinese ambassador to Germany, saying that Daimler regretted its mistake, and that it had never intended to question China's sovereignty or territorial integrity. Nor would it support anyone who deliberately undermined Chinese territorial claims. The letter's content was then published in the Chinese media. It is hard to imagine a more obsequious move: The CEO of one of the world's largest automakers apologizes twice to the Chinese government simply because one of his company's many thousands of advertising images featured a completely harmless quote from someone the Communist Party deems to be a foe. This depicts the submission of one of the world's leading car companies—caught in the trade trap.

Two weeks later, Chinese businessman Li Shufu announced that he had acquired almost 10 percent of Daimler. Possibly a coincidence. This event is symbolic proof of an insight that actually needs no proof: The West's growing economic dependence on China inevitably means increased Chinese political influence in the heart of Europe and America.

Another example epitomizes the whole dilemma: In a conversation I had in 2019 with the CEO of a large German mobility company, I asked him about his most important strategic priority for the next five years. His answer stuns me to this day. The most critical concern was to find a Chinese anchor investor and to ensure the company's economic prosperity is in the interests of the Chinese state. For that if it isn't, the company will be finished, taking a hundred thousand jobs down with it.

A BBC interview with Volkswagen CEO Herbert Diess tells a similar story. The VW CEO is asked about the company's car plant in the Xinjiang region, home to millions of Uyghurs, and his position on human rights violations in China, especially in the Uyghur camps. The transcript reads as follows:

Reporter: "And are you proud to be associated with what China is doing in this part of the world?"

Diess: "No. But we are absolutely proud to also create workplaces in that region, which we think is very useful."

Reporter: "But Xinjiang is something you're not proud to be associated with in terms of what the Chinese government is doing to the Uyghur people?"

Diess: "I can't judge this. Sorry."

Reporter: "You can't judge it?"

Diess: "No."

Reporter: "But you know about it?"

Diess: "I don't know what you're referring to."

Reporter: "You don't know about China's re-education camps for a million Uyghur people that it has referred to as re-education camps as part of its counterterror threat in the west of this country? You don't know about that?"

Diess: "I'm not aware of that."

The longer business leaders in the West think, despite all these warning signs, that they should keep doing business with China in the current way, the higher the price will be. Dependence. Ethical failure. Economic failure. Personal risk. National security risk. And finally: the breakdown of democracy. All of this goes far beyond car companies. As NATO secretary general Jens

Stoltenberg put it in January 2023: "Business is too serious to be left to business leaders alone."

Without China, many major United States tech corporations would no longer be able to provide their services. In 2020, almost half of Apple's two hundred core suppliers were located in China and Taiwan. The largest and most important is Foxconn, which employs more than a million people. There have also been frequent reports of human rights violations in the Apple supply chain.

It's no coincidence that Apple seems to operate relatively unhindered in China. According to the online publication *The Information*, Apple CEO Tim Cook signed a contract with the Chinese government that committed Apple to boosting local economies through its use of regional suppliers—in return for key legal exemptions.

Bloomberg summarizes Apple's dependence on China as follows: "The real bottleneck in production is the assembly process, better known within Apple and the manufacturing field as FATP. That stands for final assembly, test, and pack. The vast majority of Apple devices go through that process in China. That's why your MacBook Pro, iPad, or iPhone probably says, 'Assembled in China.' It's a model that Cook pioneered himself, centralizing assembly in the country as components get shipped in from around the world." Recurring pandemic lockdowns made this problematic, as factories were sometimes shut down for weeks at a time. Apple has also become more deferential to China. Following Nancy Pelosi's visit to Taiwan, it pressured its Taiwanese suppliers to avoid "Made in Taiwan" labels and to replace them with "Made in Taiwan, China," or "Made in Chinese Taipei" when shipping to China, so that there wouldn't be any production delays. The

Taiwan flag emoji has long been unavailable in China and Hong Kong. Apple headquarters in Cupertino seems very worried that China will at some point give it the big thumbs-down. So worried, in fact, that Apple began production of the new iPhone 14 in India next to China in September 2022.

Other tech companies are also wrestling with problems in China. Amazon withdrew its Chinese marketplace in 2019—after a fifteen-year stint—but continues to operate as a cloud provider through its subsidiary AWS. Facebook was blocked by China back in 2009 and, despite Mark Zuckerberg's best efforts, remains blocked. Google pulled out of the Chinese market in 2010 after some of its content was censored. Microsoft continues to operate its Bing search engine in China. However, its newly released AI bot ChatGPT was censored from Chinese big tech's services amid fears of American propaganda and uncensored replies.

China is also using infrastructure projects to create multiple dependencies in other parts of the world. Many African countries are heavily in debt, much of it incurred through participation in China's "Belt and Road Initiative," the so-called New Silk Road. In Central Africa in particular, China controls vital commodities— notably raw materials. When I asked Africa's biggest mining entrepreneur a few years ago whether America or China would end up dominating Africa as an economic power, he didn't really get my question. In Africa, he said, Chinese dominance had long been accepted as a fact of daily life.

Italy, Greece, and other Western countries have also grown increasingly dependent on China. Montenegro, for example, borrowed roughly a billion euros from China to build a quarter of a highway. That's the equivalent of more than a quarter of the Eastern European country's GDP. This is totalitarian capitalism taken to a new, international level.

The Xi regime has weaponized trade a number of times, including in the EU when tiny Lithuania dared to defy Beijing by forging links with Taiwan in 2021, China imposed a comprehensive ban on its exports, and then went a step further by threatening all European companies that manufactured goods in Lithuania with similar sanctions.

Equally, the Australian prime minister's suggestion that there should be an impartial and objective investigation into the causes of the COVID-19 pandemic was enough for Beijing to impose massive punitive tariffs on Australian wine, meat, barley, cotton, coal, seafood, and other goods. Since China was the largest export market for many of these products, this created conflict between numerous Australian companies and their home government. Beijing was already angered by new Australian legislation against foreign interference, which aimed to curb corruption and the coercion of Australian politicians and political parties. The latter had become rampant in recent years, and was largely carried out by Chinese intelligence agents and their proxies.

This Australian legislation—the National Security Legislation Amendment (Espionage and Foreign Interference) Act of 2018—is a model for how democratic countries should address the challenge of Chinese political interference without allowing xenophobia or unfair attacks on ethnic Chinese communities. It specifically aims to protect Chinese diaspora communities in Australia, who are always the first to be targeted by Chinese operatives.

The lessons learned from these sobering experiences are so

far surprisingly limited. Europe only just dodged a dependency on China in relation to 5G technology—and it seems that the EU, and particularly Germany, has a strange urge to forge ties with authoritarian states when it comes to key technologies. A fast 5G mobile network is essential for technological progress. It is the prerequisite for a modern digital infrastructure, for communication, and especially for self-driving cars. Countries without 5G will find it difficult to keep up economically. In order to make 5G available nationwide, networks will have to be extensively upgraded. To this end, thousands of masts will have to be built or converted from 4G to 5G. In sum: 5G is an essential part of every nation's infrastructure.

The world's leading provider of this technology is the Chinese company Huawei. In Europe, only Nokia and Sony Mobile (formerly known as Sony Ericsson) are able to keep up with it to some extent. For a long time, Huawei, of all companies, was Germany's preferred supplier and partner for 5G technology. Warnings, especially from the United States, were repeatedly waved away, and the fact that Huawei has been accused of corporate espionage was ignored. And yet: Everyone knows how closely the state and the economy are interwoven in China. While Huawei is nominally a private company, the Chinese security authorities legally have full access to its data.

Chinese legislation requires all companies to cooperate fully with the state's various intelligence services and to keep this cooperation absolutely secret. There is actually no such thing as a "private" company in today's China: The CCP exerts control over the whole economy and requires all CEOs to serve the Party. Huawei's founder, Ren Zhengfei, is a former military officer who has always made it clear that his main task is to work for the Party and the nation.

German infrastructure already contains a lot of Huawei technology—for example, the mobile network used by Deutsche Bahn (Germany's national railway company), as well as older radio masts. The level of Huawei's future involvement is particularly critical because 5G is more dependent on software than previous generations, which offers a bigger gateway for espionage.

Nevertheless, for a long time the German government was reluctant to exclude Huawei or the use of its components in the construction of the 5G network. The Chancellor's Office under Angela Merkel, in particular, kept postponing its decision, and was leaning toward choosing Huawei as a partner—not least to avoid straining relations with China. As late as December 2019, Merkel rejected the "exclusion of a company in principle." By this point, countries such as Japan, New Zealand, Australia, and the United States had all ruled out the company for strategic security reasons.

Today, Germany and other EU countries that were considering opting for Huawei have finally changed course. It looks like the installation of key components from Huawei will be banned. Even the use of components that have already been installed may end up being prohibited. Without American intervention, Europe under German leadership would have slid voluntarily into an irreversible dependency due to the critical need for 5G—with disastrous consequences for data security. China, with the friendly assistance of state-controlled company Huawei, almost managed to create a window for Beijing to spy on the heart of the EU.

As this case shows, it may be late in the day for the West to reset its relationship with China. The fact that the German government is repeating the mistakes of the past and selling part of the strategically important port of Hamburg to Chinese investors is also counterproductive. But a correction of that policy needs to happen.

The United States won't accept subservience to an undemocratic system without a fight. A gradual or possibly faster decoupling from China is thus a done deal (perhaps also because the United States suspects it might be cut loose otherwise). All of that is right and proper. But how? And can the United States successfully pull it off alone?

Bill Clinton promoted China's admission to the WTO. And Barack Obama's presidency is another emblem of that pivot towards the Pacific. He offered China closer relations at the beginning of his term in office, probably because China had invested enormous sums during the financial crisis and saved the global economy from collapse. "The relationship between the United States and China will shape the twenty-first century," he said in July 2009 at the opening of the U.S.-China Strategic and Economic Dialogue in Washington, while also addressing critical issues such as human rights and high energy consumption. That same year, he refrained from hosting the Dalai Lama so as to avoid provoking the Chinese leadership. Over time, however, the relationship became increasingly strained. Flashpoints included China's establishment of naval bases in the disputed and strategically important South China Sea. But there was no real resistance from Washington at this point.

Donald Trump, on the other hand, has been a long-standing challenger of China's unfair practices, especially intellectual property theft and American companies' lack of access to the Chinese market. A major goal of his presidency was to reduce the United States trade deficit with China. Yet China's dubious practices are not entirely to blame for this deficit. The United States has always imported more from China than it exports there.

Shortly after Trump became president, he sidestepped the WTO agreements and imposed tariffs on China for 2018. Since China's admission to the WTO, the Office of the United States Trade Representative (USTR) has been submitting an annual report to Congress that looks at China's WTO compliance—including all multilateral and bilateral commitments to the United States. The findings were—and still are today—alarming. Based on the USTR report and research on technology transfers and intellectual property, Trump further restricted Chinese access to investment in the high-tech sector. In response, China retaliated with its own tariffs, and accused the United States government both of triggering the trade war and trying to slow China's growth.

This makes the continuation of the decoupling policy during Joe Biden's administration all the more surprising. United States rhetoric and diplomacy have become milder and more authoritative, but their strategic substance in this area is strikingly similar to Biden's predecessor: Punitive tariffs against China have remained almost unchanged. Biden even stepped up the pace slightly by compiling a blacklist of sixty Chinese companies in 2020—which he has continuously updated since then—that United States firms may no longer do business with. Shortly afterward, the United States joined the EU, Canada, and the UK in imposing sanctions on Chinese officials in connection with human rights abuses in Xinjiang. Following the Russian invasion of Ukraine, the United States called on China to condemn the attack. China in turn blamed the United States for the war. A few weeks later, in May 2022, Chinese authorities and state-affiliated companies were told to replace American-made computers with domestic brands. Around fifty million computers were affected.

In August 2022—just days after House Speaker Nancy Pelosi's

visit to Taiwan—President Biden signed the "CHIPS and Science Act" into law, which promised $52 billions' worth of subsidies to the United States semiconductor industry. In addition, it promised tax relief for companies that expand their business in the United States. The aim is to reduce American dependence on Asia for key goods. Already in January 2022, chip manufacturer Intel had announced that it would increase America's share of global chip production from 12 percent to 30 percent within ten years.

A decoupling strategy is now taking shape in the United States. But two things are clear: Going at it alone will be tricky and decoupling itself is not enough. China is too big an economic power. That's why a strategic alliance and a common strategy is urgently needed.

Meanwhile, in Europe, the question is still "whether" not "how" more independence should be achieved—though the "whether" has been challenged by Emmanuel Macron in an heavily criticized interview with *POLITICO* after his visit to China. To him, "Europe must resist pressure to become 'America's followers'" and focus on becoming a strategically autonomous "third superpower." The hope is that Europe can perhaps muddle through—which is as opportunistic as it is naïve. It would be like trying to carry water on both shoulders: The transatlantic economic axis and defense alliance NATO on one shoulder, and European-Chinese friendship and trade relations on the other. This is a European pipe dream that will never be fulfilled. German chancellor Olaf Scholz is still convinced that a strategic trade independence from China is impossible, and that a transatlantic axis to deal with the issue is therefore unnecessary. This position will become increasingly untenable in the coming years. The question of whether and how it is revised will shape the new world order.

Europe needs to make up its mind, and a great deal will hang on its decision. Not simply democracies' prosperity, but our whole way of life. Some recent movements go in the right direction. Like the EU's reassessment of its China strategy, aiming to be bolder and more focused on economic security, as announced by Ursula von der Leyen ahead of her visit to China in spring 2023.

In the West, there are quite a few who talk down our dependence on China. Yes, China is incredibly successful, they say, but that won't last long. They point to China's ailing state banks, its excessive debts, the shift in demographics. "At the end of the day, people don't want to believe that China can be successful, because it's not a market economy based on fundamental civil rights," says Jens Südekum, German economist and professor at the Düsseldorf Institute for Competition Economics. Instead, people want to believe that a market economy is a prerequisite for sustained economic success.

The problem is: Centrally controlled, turbo-charged state capitalism can actually be more successful than a free market economy. Totalitarian capitalism is faster and more ruthless. Securing approval for a new airport can take years or even decades in a democracy, because citizen action and petitions slow things down. But managed state capitalism doesn't bother with any of that. The will of the government instantly becomes capitalist reality. Beijing's new airport was built in just under five years. If a building got in the way of the new project, then it was simply demolished. Nondemocratic power can make things faster and more efficient. And given this, arguing that China's growth will somehow just fizzle out is dangerous. It cannot be used to justify Western inaction.

Escalating economic influence eventually creates political

dependence. This means that Western entrepreneurs, CEOs, and politicians will be forced to accept standards and methods that contrast sharply with our own laws and values. The lesson for Europe is clear and should not come too late: If we continue asymmetric trading and deepening our economic relations with China, we will increasingly have to act at home—in our (still) democratic economies—in ways that avoid hurting Chinese sensitivities or disappointing Chinese expectations. The outcome? Bit by bit, our democratic systems will be eroded by an undemocratic economic superpower. In the end, that means harmonization, conformity, and subjugation. Or to put it another way: Democracies dependent on China won't stay democracies for long. They will die in the trade trap.

A Visit to Alibaba—
Jack Ma Falls Silent

On May 9, 2018, we—a group of Axel Springer leaders—pull up at the Hangzhou headquarters of Alibaba, the Chinese Amazon. The building's architecture is spectacular, like a futuristic spaceship. The silvery, shimmering façade, with its latticed organic design, looks like the wings of a giant dragonfly. Twenty-two thousand employees work here. Everything is state-of-the-art. Employees undergo facial recognition for identification purposes. Payments can be made with Alipay via cellphone throughout the company. And every single thing that employees do is monitored, documented, and controlled.

After various presentations on Alibaba's AI projects and possible collaboration avenues between our publishing group and the Chinese flagship company, we head to another building, eager for the highlight of the day: lunch with Jack Ma. On the way, we visit an exhibition telling the story of the company and its legendary founder's unique role. A photo gallery shows Ma the tai chi expert. The philosophy of tai chi is explained, and an impressive series of shots captures Grandmaster Ma in action.

As we reach the large cafeteria, we're greeted almost casually by Ma himself, a small, slim, wiry man, whose round face is filled with a wide, almost childlike smile. We enter a huge hall and as soon as Ma is spotted, employees flock to him in droves. They follow their boss around like groupies, emitting shrill cries like a girl or boy band's hysterical fans. Ma smilingly lets it all happen. It seems to be a ritual. The founder is a hugely admired star, an idol, but one you can actually touch.

We eat lunch in a kind of glass cube within the cafeteria. Everyone can watch the boss from the outside. Ma speaks perfect English. He seems calm and mild-mannered. He's considered the most Western of Chinese entrepreneurs, the one most distanced from the state—though all Chinese companies of this size ultimately have strong ties to the Party. Some say it's all a façade, that Ma is a loyal Communist apparatchik. I somehow don't want to believe this during our relaxed lunch in Hangzhou. He seems authentic to me, inwardly free. At some point between the vegetable rice and the honey shrimp, I ask: What do you think of Jeff Bezos' plan to open up space with his Blue Origin project? To which Ma replies dryly, Let Jeff take care of the orbit. I take care of planet Earth. A few months later, Ma announces his withdrawal from all operational roles at Alibaba.

In October 2020, Jack Ma, one of the richest people in the world and one of the very richest Chinese citizens, publicly criticized China's economic system. The financial system isn't a system and there are too many regulations, he reportedly said. On November 3, 2020, the IPO of Alibaba's subsidiary, Ant, was canceled by the Shanghai stock exchange—just ahead of its scheduled date—even though it had been given the green light a week before. Then, for two months, Jack Ma completely disappeared from view. Rumors varied: He'd been forced to go into hiding, he'd been living abroad, he'd been kidnapped. From that point on, he was hardly seen in public until an unexpected visit to Hangzhou in March 2023—an orchestrated show of faith in the Chinese tech sector. Ma was the first Chinese oligarch to openly make critical remarks about the regime. And here too the Communist Party has remained true to its recipe for success. Quell opposition early, discipline through deterrence, control through intimidation. Jack Ma has fallen silent.

PART IV

THE ANSWER: FREEDOM TRADE

THE DOWNFALL OF THE WORLD TRADE ORGANIZATION

Freedom and economic success are closely intertwined. One is usually a precondition of the other. As a general rule, the less free an economic system is, the less successful it will be. China is the big exception here, because what we're dealing with is state-controlled turbo-capitalism.

The WTO is built on the twin pillars of liberalism and free trade. It describes itself on its website as follows: "The World Trade Organization is the only global international organization dealing with the rules of trade between nations. At its heart are the WTO agreements, negotiated and signed by the bulk of the world's trading nations and ratified in their parliaments. The goal is to ensure that trade flows as smoothly, predictably and freely as possible."

Anyone reading this self-portrait might think that the WTO manages to avoid or satisfactorily solve all the problems outlined in this book. This, at least, is its claim. But the reality is pretty much the opposite. Under the cover of "free trade," China has used its membership to continue expanding its power by unfair means. It turns out that the WTO isn't the solution, but a fundamental part of the problem. By accelerating the weakening of truly free economies, it has fostered the rise of unfree and nondemocratic actors. It promotes dependencies and has become a Trojan horse of unfree trade.

The WTO was founded in Marrakesh in 1994 and began operating on January 1 of the following year. Its establishment led to rules being introduced for services and intellectual property. Previously, international trade rules for goods had been laid down by the General Agreement on Tariffs and Trade (GATT). The GATT treaty came into being in 1947 with the support of 23 nations. By 1994, 128 countries had joined.

GATT was created following World War II as a kind of Western club aimed at preventing a replay of the tariff wars of the 1920s. However, what began as a lean and effective collaboration between Western nations grew into the larger, ineffectual WTO we know today. It now needs a complete conceptual rethink. A GATT 2.0 of democratic nations.

WTO members pledge to observe three basic principles when forging international trade relations: trade without discrimination, reciprocity as a basis for negotiation, and the elimination of tariffs and trade barriers. Member states must therefore extend the same advantages to one another. Nondiscrimination further stipulates that the benefits and support granted to one country must automatically be granted to all member states.

However, the WTO grants special provisions to countries that define themselves as "developing"—a classification for which the organization does not provide a formal definition. Members self-declare as "developing," as China did when joining the trade alliance. The advantages include longer deadlines for implementing commitments or easier market access, among others. But the most important concession is the obligation of other WTO members to safeguard the interests of developing countries when imposing certain national or international measures—all benefits to which China has been holding on tightly since the day of its accession.

Additionally, China has repeatedly violated WTO rules for years. The list is long: forced technology transfer; massive, often undisclosed subsidies; distortion of competition by state-owned enterprises.

In order to gain access to the Chinese market, many foreign companies have had to disclose valuable technological information. The resulting cost to international businesses runs into the billions. Meanwhile, Chinese competitors in some sectors have quickly caught up with industry innovators and become market leaders themselves.

An almost traumatic example—especially for Germany—is that of photovoltaic or solar power systems. Until 2005, this industry did not exist in China. By 2022, China's share in all manufacturing stages had topped 80 percent. The GW Solar Institute at George Washington University concluded that Chinese solar production was supported by state subsidies of at least $42 billion between 2010 and 2012 alone. China's massive overproduction of solar panels triggered dramatic price drops in the sector, causing the majority of non-Chinese manufacturers to go out of business—or be bought up by their Chinese competitors.

China views Europe as a self-service shop. With great finesse, it buys into cutting-edge technology, often via "hidden champions" that are less publicly visible than companies such as Daimler, VW, or Volvo. At the height of the 2016 takeover wave, China bought up or invested in forty-four German companies alone.

Chinese antitrust laws—and especially its Anti-Monopoly Law—also have some remarkable features. China likes to punish foreign companies in particular for being innovative. Anyone who owns a patent and charges licensing royalties for its use can be classified as a monopolist by the government. Among others, smartphone manufacturer Qualcomm has been affected: It had to pay a fine of almost $1 billion for allegedly demanding excessive royalties from a Chinese competitor. Investigations in the United States and Europe reached a different conclusion.

Last but not least, China hasn't opened up its markets nearly as much as is often claimed. International companies were unable to fully access its financial sector until 2021. And a lack of transparent rules means that hardly any business can be done. There have been no successful joint ventures between Chinese and foreign companies in the telecommunications sector. Facebook and Twitter have been banned since 2009.

These examples would be scarcely imaginable the other way around. Chinese companies get to do business largely unhindered in Western markets, while the People's Republic continues to write the rule book within its own borders in ways that primarily further its own expansion of power. The WTO's own rules and those who enforce them are unable or unwilling to prevent this. Its principle of reciprocity thus remains a pious hope. In reality, the WTO is breaking down because it tolerates double standards and allows members to play by different sets of rules. Asymmetry reigns instead of reciprocity.

Nowhere is the essence of this wrongheaded, negligent

trade and economic policy so clearly reflected as in these crucial, sobering figures from the World Bank: In 2001, the year China was admitted to the WTO, America's contribution to global GDP was 31.47 percent. Two decades later, in 2021, it had fallen to 24.15 percent. Europe's share was 21.99 percent in 2001, and only 17.79 percent twenty years on. Since acquiring WTO membership, China's contribution to global GDP has risen from 3.98 percent to 18.32 percent in 2021. Furthermore, Chinese companies have overtaken global rankings accounting for 136 of all Fortune Global 500 companies in 2022. That's eleven times more than in 2001. In contrast, 54 U.S. companies have dropped out of the ranking during that same period of time. Today, only 124 remain on that list.

Looking into the future in its 2023 World Economic League Table, CEBR expects that by 2037—one year after China is set to surpass the U.S. in economic terms—China will make 21.97 percent of the world's GDP, closely followed by the U.S. with 21.71 percent and Europe's 19 percent.

CO_2 emissions are another variable that has dramatically grown for China since its accession to the WTO: They've increased by over 300 percent. And this increase offsets the rest of the world's decrease by far. China accounted for 32.87 percent of global CO_2 emissions in 2021. That's more than the United States (13.5 percent), India (7.3 percent), Russia (4.74 percent), Japan (2.88 percent), and Iran (2.02 percent)—the subsequent five largest polluters—combined. Bottom line, the global climate crisis reinforces the need to take a stand against autocratic systems like China. The real problem with climate change is not the holiday flight to Florida or Mallorca. Global air traffic accounts for only 2 percent of all carbon emissions. The problem is that we have little to no influence over the world's largest CO_2 polluter. That it pursues a completely different political agenda. And last, but not least, that we ourselves contribute to it by outsourcing the climate sins we don't want in our own backyards to China or elsewhere.

Viewed from today's perspective, China's admission as a full member of the WTO was a fundamental error in a trade policy led by wishful thinking. Motivated, as so often, by good intentions, it created an imbalance that has worsened down the years, much to the detriment of democratic market economies. The main mistake was giving entry to an economically weighty, nondemocratic state, which, due to its own outlook, was unable to adhere to free trade rules. The most ridiculous mistake was to grant China the developing country status—which it still has today despite being the second largest economy in the world. With all the exceptions and exemptions that come with it. It's like granting privileges to the most ruthless kid on the block. Competition couldn't be more unfair or masochistic.

The result of this experiment was predictable: In the short term it brought growth and economic success to all participants, but in the long term it shifted the balance in ways that allowed dependencies and one-sided advantages to emerge. The masochism of the United States and Europe, in particular, led not only to a weakening of their own relative economic power, but also in the end to an erosion of the entire WTO. And speaking of the end: The WTO has reached the end of the line. What we see before us now is a dysfunctional and paralyzed colossus—a shadow of its former self.

The United States has enormously contributed to this state of affairs. Ever since the Obama administration, the United States has blocked the appointment of judges to the WTO's Appellate Body, citing concerns over its jurisprudence. Normally, when the WTO makes a decision regarding a trade dispute, the losing country need only refer it to the Appellate Body; historically, two out of three cases have been decided on appeal. Right now, however, appeals cannot be processed because the body simply isn't quorate. The United States, moreover, ceased its payments to the Appellate Body in 2017.

All of which leads to the unsparing conclusion: The WTO should be dissolved.

Dinner with the Ambassador— And Why the Chinese Feel Very Hurt

On June 11, 2018, some colleagues and I are invited to dine with Shi Mingde, the Chinese ambassador in Berlin. The invitation was prompted by a trip we'd just made to China to find out more about Chinese tech innovation. We firmly believe that China, which has been copying American and European patents and innovations for decades, is now a leader in the field of AI—as demonstrated by the meteoric rise of companies like Tencent, Alibaba, and ByteDance. The Chinese Embassy had helped us organize the trip, and we now want to share our experiences with the ambassador.

Shi welcomes us to one of the most beautiful villas in Grunewald, a leafy residential area of Berlin. The magnificent Wilhelmine property appears to have been extensively renovated. Our convivial host shows us to a be-columned veranda overlooking a garden with a perfectly manicured lawn. After enjoying an apéritif and chatting a bit about German politics, we head inside and take our seats at a round table. We eat various Chinese delicacies with chopsticks. And drink white wine. Followed by rice liquor.

The conversation is mostly benign. We thank him for his kind support in organizing the trip, and tell him how impressed we were by some of the companies we visited in Beijing, Shenzhen, and Hangzhou. The ambassador's self-confidence is striking. Something in the overall tone has changed. Twenty years ago, the Chinese ambassador would have thanked German visitors for their interest in his country. No longer. Now this world power receives visitors from the West with a friendly but somewhat regal air.

The ambassador wonders if such a visit might lead to rather more positive reporting about the land of progress and prosperity. We courteously explain our principle of editorial independence and the decision-making rules in place between our editors and the management team. Our host's expression is filled first with astonishment, then with pity.

Toward the end of the meal, I make a point of raising the "Mercedes and Dalai Lama" incident, which saw the Daimler CEO apologize for a Mercedes ad that used a Dalai Lama quote. The ambassador is happy to discuss it in detail. The ad caused tremendous upset in China, he says. To the government? I ask. No, to the people, says the ambassador—the Chinese media had reported the matter extensively. I diplomatically resist commenting that the Chinese media probably only reported it extensively because the Communist Party made sure that they reported it extensively. Then I ask: Was it really necessary for Daimler's CEO to apologize twice to the Chinese government and people for the ad? Or was this actually a case of anticipatory obedience? Barely skipping a beat, the ambassador puts on his very friendliest smile and says in a mild, singsong voice, No, the CEO certainly didn't need to apologize. Unless—and here he deliberately inserts a little pause—unless Mercedes wishes to continue selling cars in China. Then of course Mr. Zetsche did need to apologize. Because the Chinese people felt very hurt by this ad.

We have another glass of rice liquor, thank him for the enlightening meal, and then say our goodbyes.

The ambassador briefly waves us off. His expression is still a mixture of astonishment and pity.

THE CONTRACT—
A NEW WORLD TRADE ORDER

We need a new world trade order. The creation of a new alliance that provides a multinational framework for truly free trade. An economic alliance of democracies: **the Freedom Trade**.

This alliance will have simple, clear, and nonnegotiable criteria for accession. Only countries that meet its rules may become members. Only countries that comply with its rules may remain members. The three key criteria are:

1. **Adherence to the rule of law**
2. **Adherence to human rights**
3. **Adherence to CO_2 targets**

Alliance members will be able to engage in truly free trade without any tariffs or restrictions. Nonmembers will be allowed to trade with members, but will be subject to high tariffs.

The Freedom Trade Alliance will be forged in a community of shared values. An alliance of economies that adhere to the same democratic principles: respect for the rule of law, for human rights, and for sustainability. The underlying hypothesis is that cooperation between democratic states leads to more value creation than partnerships with autocracies. This alliance will strengthen democratic economies and thus democracy itself. Its long-term success will far outweigh initial costs and risks. The entire model is based on incentives rather than prohibitions.

The alliance avoids dependencies on rapidly expanding autocratic or nondemocratic economies and their political systems. The alliance avoids political interference and infiltration, the weakening of free societies, and the subsequent destruction of democracy by dictatorships and autocracies.

The alliance avoids deglobalization and promotes international cooperation—among truly democratic allies.

Opportunistic economic and trade policies without shared values have failed in the same way as socialism. The existing trade trap will be replaced by a values-based trade policy that will secure and shape a democratic world order.

First, let's look at the three fundamental criteria in more detail.

The rule of law is a proven concept, one that is clearly defined but whose nuances have been interpreted in various ways. The definition goes back to the Greek philosopher Aristotle. It describes the principle that all people and organizations within a country, state, or community are held accountable to the same set of laws. It is vital that the Freedom Trade Alliance's rule-of-law criteria are as simple and basic as possible. It's about making the club of democratic Freedom Trade members as large and attractive as possible. Those that credibly fulfill and maintain the key criteria of a constitutional state are welcome. These criteria include the provision of legal certainty and equality of rights, judicial control, the separation of powers, and safeguarding freedom. Or, to put it in another way: no power abuse on the part of the state; independent courts; a binding constitution; equal treatment before the law.

The criteria listed by independent think tank Freedom House in its "Freedom in the World" report can serve as a starting point. These are used to measure the relative freedom of countries in an annual report, first published in 1973. Each country and territory is scored on: political pluralism and participation, electoral process, functioning of government, rule of law, and individual rights such as the right to self-determination as well as freedom of expression, belief, assembly, and association. The country is then classified as "Free," "Partly Free," or "Not Free." As such, members of the Freedom Trade Alliance are only to be classified as "Free" or "Partly Free" countries.

The Freedom Trade human rights criteria will also contain fundamental values and requirements: No one should be subjected to discrimination or persecution due to their skin color, religion, political views, sexual orientation, or gender. These rights could be defined based on the U.N.'s Universal Declaration of Human Rights. Every human being has the right to liberty. Torture and slavery are prohibited. Everyone has the right to a trial and to be presumed innocent. Everyone has the right to vote, the right to education, the right to property, and freedom of religion. The criteria for the rule of law and human rights are but a stone's throw apart—and often overlap. Experts need to configure the exact requirements. The core message of Freedom Trade is: Only those who respect human rights, sustainability, and democracy may join the alliance. Anyone who refuses must accept high tariffs—so high that there is a strong incentive for change.

The climate targets will be based on clear and synchronized commitments to reduce CO_2 emissions—building on existing concepts like the "climate club," a collaborative initiative established by the G7 countries in 2022 to strengthen the implementation of the Paris Agreement. The key issue is reaching a joint agreement on a price for CO_2 emissions. This would be supplemented by CO_2 border tariffs: Anyone wishing to import goods into the Freedom Trade area would pay a surcharge depending on how much CO_2 is embedded in a product. In addition, common rules should be established on how, for instance, the CO_2 content of products and materials is measured. Collaborative research projects and initiatives would develop joint solutions on how, for example, energy-intensive industries can lower their CO_2 emissions more quickly.

Applying these criteria to the world's largest and most influential economies leads to the following picture: In 2021, based on the World Bank data model, the top fifty GDP contributors accounted for 93.13 percent of global GDP. Cross-referencing these fifty countries against Freedom House's 2023 "Freedom in the World Report" gives the following result: Among the top fifty GDP-contributing countries, nine are classified as "Not Free," eleven as "Partly Free," and thirty as "Free." Thus, the countries rated as "Free" in the top fifty accounted for 60.17 percent of global GDP in 2021. If the "Partly Free" countries are included—like India, Mexico, or Indonesia—the total is 69.08 percent. The "Not Free" countries—such as China, Russia, or Saudi Arabia—contributed 24.05 percent. This shows that the majority of the economies in this model continue to adhere to democratic principles and also to account for most of global GDP.

At the moment, democracies still have the upper hand. Our task now is to safeguard that. The Freedom Trade Alliance—by achieving a critical mass through its values-based appeal and material benefits—has a genuine chance of becoming the catalyst for a new world trade and political order.

The WTO has failed. There's no point in clinging to it in either its current or a restructured form. Our best chance is to start afresh, a true reset of the GATT agreement. Of course, today's agreement must be more comprehensive. Back then, it was "only" about tariffs. Today, far more (trade) aspects have to play a role from the outset, such as foreign direct investments, intellectual property, market access, and more. The architecture of the organization needs to be as minimalistic and as unbureaucratic as possible.

The Freedom Trade Alliance has at least forty potential founding countries. The United States and Europe must take the lead—forming the basis of a truly transatlantic strategy. Canada, Australia, Japan, Mexico, and more could swiftly follow. African countries, which are not yet fully dependent on China, could quickly be won over. Gaining India as a member would be particularly important. And one day, even today's non-democracies might be drawn by the magnet of prosperity through freedom. It may seem a utopian vision, but even Russia and China might join the Freedom Trade Alliance one day in the future.

How should it be structured? I would like to see experts, students, and engaged citizens working together to generate concrete ideas for implementation—true crowdsourcing to discuss the details of the model and the best ways of turning it into reality. The purpose of this book is not to go into the details of political governance—experts know better. This is not a recipe, it is about an idea.

We need a new beginning built on the core principle that successful free trade between countries is rooted in the freedom of their societies. In the long run, trade without shared basic values and goals won't result in added value. Above all, this kind of trade creates dependencies and political interference from bad actors. Only if the rules apply equally to everyone will we see fair competition and fair results for all.

Focusing on environmental, social, and governance (ESG) principles as the new criteria for a modern and responsible way to do business, while simultaneously outsourcing ever more business—so as to cut costs and boost growth—in countries that fundamentally breach these criteria is a cynical and ultimately dysfunctional strategy.

Of course, the Freedom Trade approach also involves numerous risks, disadvantages, and tensions. Developing countries are currently growing faster than industrialized nations. And a large proportion of developing countries are not (yet) democratic. In

2020, the first year of the COVID-19 pandemic, a large majority of the fifty largest economies reported negative growth. Only seven countries bucked the trend with positive growth rates: Ireland, Egypt, Bangladesh, Iran, Vietnam, China, and Turkey, out of which merely two, Ireland and Bangladesh, are respectively classified as "Free" and "Partly Free." Among the ten largest economies, China was the only one that made a gain. By 2021, the macroeconomic situation had eased and most countries were reporting growth again. However, when you look at growth rates as a whole, the same trend emerges: Nondemocratic states are growing disproportionately compared to democracies. Initially, committing to the conditions of the new democratic trade alliance would cause significant slumps and uncertainties in the foreign trade of member states. The shock waves would be enormous and the short-term losses substantial—but by no means intolerable. The price of that process would be much cheaper than the costs of a trade policy that's still led by shortsighted opportunism.

In the wake of Russia's invasion of Ukraine and the economic upheavals it has caused—which have affected Germany more than any other country—the Leibniz Institute for Economic Research (ifo Institute) at the University of Munich set up a study called "Geopolitical Challenges and Their Consequences for the German Economic Model" ("*Geopolitische Herausforderungen und ihre Folgen für das deutsche Wirtschaftsmodell*"). The study analyzes and quantifies future scenarios in which democratic blocs completely decouple from China. It assumes an orderly approach—that all actors would behave rationally (which is by no means self-evident or likely)—and calculates the medium- to long-term effects after ten to twelve years. It does not take growth effects and short-term deviations into account. The figures relating to the possible negative effects are surprisingly low. But the more illustrative element of the study is its comparison of different scenarios.

According to the ifo Institute study, if the EU were to unilaterally decouple from China—calculated as one-sided tariffs on Chinese imports, Europe's GPD would fall by just under a percent point. In the case of a bilateral decoupling from China and the EU—the more realistic scenario, in which both would increase costs on imports—the slump in European GDP would amount to 1.34 percent. China would lose 0.42 percent of its GDP in the unilateral scenario and 0.76 percent in the case of a trade war. The GDP of the rest of the world would hardly be affected and even grow a little.

The toughest outcome for China would be if the EU and the United States decided to proceed in a coordinated fashion. The Leibniz Institute calculates a decline in Chinese GDP of 1.49 percent in the unilateral scenario and 2.27 percent in the bilateral one. For Europe, decoupling from China in a Western alliance would be only marginally more expensive than going solo. The United States would see a 0.40 percent decline in GDP in the unilateral case and 0.48 percent in the event of a trade war.

Besides indicating the estimated long-term effects of such a collective independence are lower than one might think, the study shows: China has much more to lose. This further leads to the assumption that the potential leverage would indeed catalyze a shift in China's behavior—"Change through no trade" or "*Wandel durch kein Handel*" as the exact antithesis of the originally claimed maxim.

A more radical set of scenarios is modeled in another study.

Economists at the *Kiel Institute for the World Economy* examined the effects of an East-West decoupling in their March 2022 paper "Cutting Through the Value Chain: The Long-Run Effects of decoupling the East from the West." One of their scenarios is closer to the idea of a Freedom Trade Alliance: decoupling the United States and the EU from the BRIC countries—Brazil, Russia, India, and China. Russia and China are clearly authoritarian. Brazil and India are classified as "Free" and "Partly Free" by Freedom House, but both countries have shown a decline in democracy in recent years. All four are among the top twelve contributors to global GDP. In this scenario, the drop in welfare (measured by real income) among alliance members would be 1.10 percent in the unilateral case of the U.S. and its allies decoupling from BRIC countries and 1.32 percent in a bilateral, trade-war case. Among BRIC countries, overall prosperity falls by between 2.75 percent (unilateral) and 3.86 percent (bilateral). However, the impact on individual countries varies. Russia would be hit hardest by a trade war with the West, with a 9.62 percent drop in prosperity, whilst Brazil, India, and China fare a little better.

This second study clearly shows: The larger the alliance of democracies, the stronger the negative effects on nondemocratic states. This is another reason why it seems sensible—in contrast to what is suggested in the study—to win Brazil and India for the Freedom Trade Alliance as soon as possible. The greater the critical mass, the less damage within democratic economies and the greater the pull effect.

Both of the studies—especially that of the Leibniz Institute—assume an orderly, rational approach and a long horizon of ten to twelve years. Things might not happen that way. And the short-term effects, specifically the disruptive impact of a values-based trade policy, naturally can't be measured in such analyses. But even if the short-term effects were more negative for the West, it would still be more sensible to proceed proactively and shape a new world trade order in a coordinated manner, rather than just waiting and hoping for miracles. The price of trade wars and conventional wars is definitely higher.

Opponents of a new values-based trade policy are likely to exaggerate its negative effects. But they have a point in being skeptical. One important example is the German automotive industry. It is already dependent on the Chinese market for around a third of its sales and in some cases for more than half of its profits. Abruptly sacrificing the Chinese market, and then Russian and undemocratic Middle Eastern markets, would threaten the very existence of the German car industry. Hundreds of thousands of jobs would be at risk. The backbone of the German economy would be broken.

Another example is the American healthcare sector. Eighty percent of antibiotics prescribed in the United States come from China or are based on ingredients sourced from China. Or take the rare earths supply chain, at the beginning of which China is playing a dominant role. Forgoing either of these abruptly or completely would have unacceptable consequences for our physical and mental health.

Simultaneously renouncing gas and oil from Russia, Saudi Arabia, and Qatar seems equally inconceivable. This would result in the collapse of the EU's energy policy—especially if some member states are naïve enough to insist that they cannot use nuclear energy or American fracked gas on ideological grounds.

Or if the expansion of renewable energies continues to be slowed by ideological debates.

Immediate and complete decoupling would also be damaging for international investments. The Chinese sovereign wealth fund, the China Investment Corporation (CIC), is one of the largest and most active investors in the world, with $1.35 trillion in assets under management, including former investments in Blackstone and Morgan Stanley. According to a report by the United States think tank Foundation for Defense of Democracies (FDD), the CIC was involved in 613 overseas transactions through its private equity investments between 2007 and 2019, 60 percent of which were in the United States, the UK, Germany, France, and the Netherlands.

That's why we need a better solution than just decoupling. The immediate implementation of a "pure" Freedom Trade strategy isn't realistic. Intermediate steps and complementary measures are required to reach the goal. These measures would offer a decisive advantage: orderly action by the newly conceived trade alliance as opposed to disorderly reactions to future trade wars or armed conflicts. In a passive scenario, countries may panic and react defensively. In a proactive scenario, democracies go on the offensive in a structured and deliberate way.

A two-step model or even a model with several more nuanced steps could well be the answer. The first step would involve limiting punitive tariffs for nondemocratic countries by applying them to critical infrastructure products and services only: semiconductors, components for solar and wind farms, robotics, biotechnology, AI solutions, communications, tech platforms. By contrast, everyday consumer goods such as clothing, toys, consumer electronics, and furniture—things that are highly important to most people but only have indirect strategic importance—could be exempt from the new rules for a transitional period of a few years. Ethical questions relating to production methods—such as child labor—are important, and should be resolved as quickly as possible, but whether or not a T-shirt was produced in China for the cheapest price won't determine global system dominance in the medium term.

However, the question of whether Europe puts itself in the hands of Huawei for 5G network expansion—and thus to a significant degree under the control of the CCP—is of central strategic and political importance. Equally, the question of how far Chinese AI platforms will shape and control the future reach of information and intellectual property. These questions have a systemic relevance, especially since individual decisions made by consumers and even business partners are steered by algorithms and are thus not truly free. Where practical alternatives are lacking, clear regulatory frameworks are needed. The U.S. and the UK are paving the way with their ban and restrictions, over security concerns, on selling and using Huawei's products.

State financial support will be a necessity for a transitional period, to shield certain industries from the negative economic effects of the shift to values-based trade. From the automotive industry and its suppliers to the energy sector to medication production—all would need state aid to make the change work. Uncontrolled disruption would hit the economies of some democracies too hard, risking dangerous centrifugal social forces such as polarization and political extremism. Special state funds for particularly affected companies and industries are thus needed to enable an orderly and successful transition. And these state funds would be an excellent investment. They wouldn't simply be a Band-Aid; they would create new, sovereign structures. The alternatives would cost much more.

The words "state aid" are rightly a red flag for many regulatory policymakers. But the idea of being able to completely forgo such support is illusory. And the recent past, in particular, has taught us that a "business as usual" approach to trade—one that creates dependencies on dictatorships—can lead to a rise in state intervention of a completely different magnitude. Russia's war and the COVID-19 pandemic are illustrations of this. In both cases, the EU and the United States haven't hesitated to dig deep into their coffers.

The German government has approved almost 300 billion euros in state aid packages for German citizens and companies affected by Russia's war of aggression. And it was also willing to use massive state subsidies to protect society from the effects of the global pandemic. During COVID-19, no sum was too high. Germany created a relief package worth 130 billion euros. In France, it was over 100 billion euros. And the EU has set up a 750-billion-euro reconstruction fund. Surely the amount we've spent protecting ourselves from a previously unknown virus isn't too big an outlay when it comes to protecting our free way of life from attack?

And while these sums may sound like a lot, they're a drop in the ocean compared to what the United States has spent. The relief bill that Joe Biden pushed through at the beginning of his term in office was worth $1.9 trillion alone. A $900 billion support program was approved in December 2020, and $2.2 trillion was released at the start of the pandemic. That's $5 trillion in total. One day, even the most die-hard apologists for the apolitical notion of business as an end in itself will be forced to realize: If values and principles keep getting sacrificed, then the foundations for conducting good business will eventually crumble. The enormous economic damage caused by Europe's reliance on Russian energy—and the bitter awakening that has accompanied it— is but the start.

All change involves risk. And it's clear that a fundamental change of approach in our trade policy would involve some losses. We need to be prepared to face these setbacks. That's why it's also important to focus on the opportunities change will bring. The political and social advantages are obvious and can be summed up in one word: sovereignty. Sovereignty means freedom. The sovereignty of democratic open societies is a precious asset, perhaps the most precious asset of all. It is worth almost any price.

But how high a price would it actually be? One percent of our GDP? Five percent? Ten percent? Is there a price that we would no longer be willing to pay? Where would we draw the line? The line is where the societal risks become so high that they endanger the very foundations of what we are fighting for: freedom and democracy.

Even the most pessimistic scenario shows that the effects of a Freedom Trade policy would be manageable. Especially if nations avoid being as reactive as they were with the Russian war on Ukraine—but are proactive instead. Our willingness to take risks will largely depend on our risk awareness. If people's "sense of urgency" is low, they prefer to leave things as they are. If their "sense of urgency" is high, their openness to change increases, along with its associated risks. The result is a trade-off. In the end, you choose the lesser of the two evils.

A realistic evaluation of the opportunities a proactive Freedom Trade strategy could bring us is just as vital as a realistic assessment of the dangers posed by our current trade strategy and the risks of making a decisive change.

In the first phase of truly democratic free trade, the production of countless goods and services that had been moved to cheaper, nondemocratic countries would make their way back to democratic markets. This would strengthen the economies of Freedom Trade Alliance members and have an enormous impact, in particular, on the labor market. Products might be more expensive to produce, but economies with higher real wages would see a boost in both their productivity and the demand for goods and services. Those on lower incomes would benefit in particular. The enormous relocation of jobs would thus have a significant impact.

Even if we see only some of the jobs move back to America and Europe, they would act as an unprecedented economic stimulus package. We now face decades of skill shortages in America and Europe. Scarcity of qualified labor is one of the biggest problems of our time. And one that can't be solved without immigration. Huge numbers of migrants and skilled professionals are needed to make this work. The Freedom Trade could be a healthy catalyst with benefits for everyone. In order to encourage relocation, countries will need to dramatically improve their immigration processes based on clear criteria, skill requirements, and educational offerings.

Members of the Freedom Trade Alliance would be allowed to do more than just trade without tariffs. Travel, tourism, and working in other member countries—the term "foreign countries" doesn't really fit anymore—would be made easier, an additional stimulus for these highly important growth sectors. All in all, the Freedom Trade Alliance and the benefits it offers member states would accelerate both global economic growth and the establishment of sustainable social and environmental standards. And by generating competition between systems, the significant structural advantages of democratic countries would also become apparent—especially since the impact on nonmembers of the Freedom Trade Alliance would be both huge and hugely negative. The United States's share of China's foreign trade was 13.6 percent in 2022. The European share was just over 20 percent. Were one of those markets to break away, China could still cope. But the simultaneous loss of the United States and the EU—affecting more than a quarter of China's foreign trade—would be almost impossible for China to offset.

Nondemocratic economies would suffer great losses in GDP and growth as a result of a fortified, values-based trade policy. They would lose—potentially in two stages—their largest and most important trading partners. Along with jobs and value creation. In the event of a bilateral decoupling of China from Europe and the United States, China would lose 2.27 percent of its GDP in the long term, according to the ifo Institute study. Measured against today's income ($17.73 trillion GDP in 2021), that's just over $400 billion. The incentives for aligning with the Freedom Trade Alliance are considerable.

Nondemocratic states would thus be confronted with a fundamental choice: whether to allow misguided pride and outdated convictions to take precedence over economic prosperity and national well-being. More concretely: Progressive economic isolation and the loss of big markets would increase the pressure for political renewal. When growth stagnates or declines, when prosperity dwindles and ever fewer citizens are able to build on the social advances of recent decades—in China or Saudi Arabia or Russia—these countries' regimes will face very clear choices. More freedom or less prosperity? Modernizing and joining the Freedom Trade Alliance or oppressing their own people? Of course, trade between nondemocratic states would significantly increase. But ultimately this wouldn't be enough to compensate for the loss of large democratic markets.

The price of oppression would be tangible for every citizen: less growth and prosperity. This would lead to higher levels of discontent among populations. And more discontent—despite repressive government rule—means more instability, up to and including uprisings and revolutions. And this will be one of the most crucial factors at the crossroads between democracy and dictatorship.

Every country is free to decide. To join or not to join. The greater the critical mass of members, the greater the incentive to participate. America on its own would not be enough. America plus Europe is a start. With each new country that joins, the likelihood of success increases exponentially. In particular, indecisive, weaker, or opportunistic countries would quickly realize that the risk of allowing more freedom and democracy is worthwhile in order to gain prosperity, growth, and security. Sooner rather than later, a number of African countries would follow the path of reason. The UAE could even act as a bridge for Freedom Trade into the Muslim world, strengthening freedom rather than giving up prosperity. Only very small, hardened dictatorial regimes like North Korea are likely to resist such changes permanently, or at least for the foreseeable future.

India—the world's most populous state—will play a crucial role in the global power balance of the future. It can either continue to pursue a path of maximum neutrality or pick a side. For years it has been trying to play at eye level with the largest economies, which might have underestimated India's relevance given its colonial past. This is changing as India forges a foreign policy of its own—much of which has to do with its military independence. For so long Russia was one of India's most trusted suppliers of weapons. In light of the war and sanctions, Russia's diminished supply ability is pushing India to forge new alliances. Winning over India to join the Freedom Trade will be one of the most impactful and strategic moves.

Saudi Arabia is a special case. On the one hand, it's a modern and important economy, and on many levels a strategic ally of the United States. And on the other, it's one of the most autocratic and ruthless Islamist regimes. America needs to make a principled decision. Particularly as the lessons from the past are clear: Friends and foes can change. One day it's Iraq, the next day Iran, the following day Egypt. But building alliances with one dictator against another has rarely paid off in the long run. A values-based trade policy means criteria that apply to everyone, rather than exceptions being made for friends. And the foes of today can become future friends in the context of Freedom Trade.

It is not inconceivable that Russia might one day join the Freedom Trade Alliance. No one knows how long such a development would take. But there will be a time after Putin. And unless there is another very surprising turn of events, this dictator will leave a devastated Russia behind him—a country that's not just economically weakened, but practically destroyed. It will be a country that now faces a more united West: a strengthened NATO, a stronger EU, a strengthened transatlantic alliance. The West will also be less dependent on gas supplies. As a result, Russia's economic foundations will collapse.

Any new government in Moscow will then have to make a key strategic choice: either to become an ally of the democratic West or to hitch its wagon to a nondemocratic China. It is precisely these *two* options that are open to Putin's successors. And therein lies a historic opportunity for a new and better world order. When the time comes, the West must resist exploiting the weakness of the loser, a post-Putin Russia. It should envisage a new, differently governed Russia. And the West could begin preparations that would allow Russia to rebuild its economy as quickly as possible, thus mounting a forceful resistance to the challenges and threats that China and Islamist states pose. From today's perspective, this idea may seem far-fetched. But if we take a longer view, one that plays out over decades, it is more likely than it looks.

Regardless of how high or low the probability of Russia joining the alliance is, we must do everything we can to increase that probability. Because all the alternatives are worse. A permanently humiliated Russia would become increasingly aggressive. A Russia permanently in thrall to China would become a powerful adversary, disadvantaging us economically and politically. And the chances of Russia choosing a better, more liberal path after its self-inflicted humiliation are, historically speaking, actually not bad. In the past, two major military defeats have prompted regime changes in Russia. The loss of the Crimean War in 1856 led to major reforms and a decline in serfdom. Defeat in the Russo-Japanese War in 1905 greatly weakened autocratic tsarism, culminating in the 1917 February Revolution and the Bolshevik October Revolution. So perhaps this is something of a pattern: Military defeats make Russia more open to change. And the West can help steer the direction this change takes.

It would be a bold and dangerous move to deny one's own people prosperity and freedom purely to stabilize one's own autocratic power. In the end, the chance of losing both would be high. In countries that have never experienced growing prosperity, leaders may still try to take this path. But some nations will find this more difficult: those that for decades have allowed large numbers of socially underprivileged people to move up into a growing middle class that enjoys the products and services of freedom. Even in China, Saudi Arabia, and Russia, too many have now come into contact with beguiling luxuries and individual freedoms. We shouldn't underestimate the appeal of our open societies. If the pursuit of happiness were to be tempered with a little more self-awareness and economic sense, autocracies would find it much harder to oppress and forcibly impoverish their own people.

The Freedom Trade Alliance will therefore play a dual role: It will act both as an incentive and as a means of exerting pressure for modernization and liberalization. And it is by no means impossible that this democratic alliance would quickly gain more members than expected.

An orderly reduction of our codependency right now is smarter than waiting on a war with China. Creating a new multinational trade alliance right now is smarter than radical and chaotic decoupling. Taking joint action right now is smarter than being reactive or going it alone. The Freedom Trade project is our best chance for securing democracy and freedom.

There will be significant resistance from numerous business leaders and investors. In their book *Hidden Hand: Exposing How the Chinese Communist Party Is Reshaping the World*, Clive Hamilton and Mareike Ohlberg describe the "shuttle diplomacy" of Wall Street banks such as Goldman Sachs, Morgan Stanley, and the Blackstone Group. Their aims were, first, to support China's admission to the WTO and, second, to maintain China-friendly United States government policies. In particular, Larry Fink, the longtime CEO of BlackRock, the world's largest investment fund, is credited with a successful lobbying role. The company's profits over the past two decades appear to confirm this strategy, but existential dangers on the horizon now mark the end of this opportunistic and shortsighted phase.

Some lead investors and industry representatives, seeing only the short-term negative effects of a Freedom Trade strategy, are bound to make fundamental objections citing regulatory policy. They will be critical of the new trade alliance's rules, which in their eyes constitute a massive restriction on economic freedom.

Of course there are restrictions. Especially as the concept of Freedom Trade can only succeed if accompanied and strengthened by so-called secondary sanctions. This means that should a company's shareholders come up with the idea of relocating to a nonmember country—for example, transferring the corporate headquarters of General Motors or VW to Beijing—the same rules would apply to these companies as to any others in nonmember states. They would effectively decouple themselves from Freedom Trade Alliance markets. The same would apply to subsidiaries and joint ventures because there is no other way to stop the alliance's rules being circumvented. Halfhearted implementation would be worse than no change. The idea works completely or not at all. It would be implemented in an orderly fashion and in stages—but it should also be consistently and effectively backed up with sanctions.

So the plan would indeed involve substantial encroachment on existing entrepreneurial freedoms. But this is to ensure long-term economic independence and the conditions for success. In other words: It is to ensure freedom and capitalism. In that context we should remember that the history of economics is littered with restrictions and new, previously unimaginable rules. If there are too many rules—and, above all, the wrong rules—the result is a planned economy, socialism, mismanagement, and failure. If there are reasonable rules, capitalistic success and social progress will follow.

Some examples: Trade unions do restrict economic freedoms. But at some point these were considered acceptable and reasonable by the majority because it was more humane—more in line with our democratic conception of humanity—than the unrestrained exploitation of a working class made defenseless by poverty. It was considered more just, but also more stable. Unrest and uprisings—like the weavers' revolts, which symbolized the discontent of poorly treated workers in the fourteenth and nineteenth centuries—have undoubtedly been prevented in this way. A balance has been established that is healthier for both sides—and more predictable than the early industrial excesses of capitalism.

Age limits, retirement ages, and pensions form another set of restrictions. Why shouldn't an entrepreneur in a free market economy employ workers until they collapse of old age? Why shouldn't everyone just have to work until he or she gets sick or drops dead? Because democratic societies have recognized that this is shameful and inhumane. Retirement ages, pension plans, and pension funds are handled very differently in America and Europe. But certain obligations and rules exist on both continents—the achievement of a modern market economy that conforms to the ethical framework of democracy.

Another restriction is the prohibition of child labor. How efficient it used to be for employers to use children—as soon as they were able—in hard physical labor, especially for lower, less demanding types of work. How cheap it was to exploit children from socially disadvantaged families at the lowest possible wages in highly dangerous conditions in quarries and mines. And yet, thankfully, child labor was recognized as wrong and brought to an end in democratic countries. Child labor has existed for millennia. It began rising in the seventeenth century and skyrocketed during the Industrial Revolution. Britain and Prussia started to severely restrict or prohibit child labor from the 1830s onward. Child labor has been banned in the United States since June 25, 1938. It is prohibited by Article 32 of the Charter of Fundamental Rights of the European Union—and has been forbidden for more than a century in many EU member states. Western democracies have decided that this form of exploitation is not in line with their values. How, then, can they allow cheap goods produced by child labor to be imported and sold in their countries—just because that child labor takes place beyond their own shores? Today, nearly one-in-ten children is working. That's 160 million worldwide, according to UNICEF and the International Labour Organization. Child labor is most prevalent in sub-Saharan Africa, with some 86.6 million children working, and in Asia-Pacific, where there are 48.7 million child laborers.

More recently, sustainability, gender equality, and diversity have further limited economic freedoms. Why shouldn't employers simply hire someone of whatever gender they prefer? Why do employers need to be tolerant and treat sexual minorities equally? Why consider the environment? These can all be viewed as limitations that restrict a purely capitalist idea of freedom. And yet, over time, democratic societies have recognized that such measures are reasonable and desirable, and have implemented them on the basis of the law, dignity, and human rights.

A century ago, such ideas had barely got off the ground, even in America and Europe. Today, we rightly see these rules and standards in a more pragmatic and less exaggerated manner, as an advance in civilization. We also understand that we can achieve far better results in a working world that is tolerant and diverse. So how can we justify trading with, or sourcing and manufacturing products in, countries where women aren't allowed to drive or are denied the right to vote? How can we do business in countries that persecute or condemn people to death simply for being gay?

Double standards don't come more glaring or unethical than this. You outsource stuff that you yourself would no longer countenance to nondemocratic countries. Along the lines of: "Where there's already injustice, what's a bit more?" The CEO who makes virtuous speeches about ESG standards in the morning and then shifts a bit more of the company's production to China or Belarus in the afternoon has no credibility. And the fact that an employee can lose their job because of a misplaced gender pronoun, but their colleague can brag about increased sales in countries where women are stoned to death for adultery, merits at least some examination. In this respect our current trade policy isn't just shortsighted. It is contradictory and bigoted. And simply unsustainable.

Finally, defenders of the status quo like to go back to fundamentals. An argument that's often advanced to prevent any change in our economic relations with China and other unjust states is that of protectionism. Reducing dependency on China or other countries through a tougher trade policy, they argue, is ultimately a form of isolationism designed to protect our own weaker markets. Protectionism is a dirty word to me, an advocate of liberal market economies and free trade. Which means that it can be weaponized to head off unwelcome developments. But first we should ask: Has American economic policy ever been completely free of protectionism? And second: Is this really about protectionism—about closing off one's own markets? It's actually the opposite. It's about preventing deglobalization. It's about strengthening international economic relations, and about genuine free trade and fair conditions for all. The aim is to reduce the imbalance that rule violations and abuses have created, and to prevent the threat of dependencies—or to deal with those that already exist. The debate is therefore not about protectionism at all, but how to protect our values and sovereignty. A new trade policy is vital to prevent the gradual infiltration and weakening of democratic market economies by autocratic forms of state capitalism. Genuine free trade—in other words, free trade that is fair—is not only more ethical, but also more successful. Conversely, there are plentiful examples of how doing business in nondemocratic countries (with its attendant risks) has caused companies immense harm:

"Those who neglect morality end up damaging profitability," former Siemens CEO Heinrich von Pierer, who sat in Chancellor Kohl's plane to China, once wrote. Sadly, Siemens ignored this wisdom. Between 1997 and 2006, the company operated a worldwide bribery scheme designed to secure orders and increase its share price. The company paid out an estimated 1.3 billion euros in countries including Algeria, Libya, Nigeria, China, and Russia. Around 4,300 payments and 330 affected projects were later identified. None of this helped Siemens. In addition to suffering vast reputational damage, the company was forced to pay billions of euros in fines, back taxes, and legal and auditing fees.

In the short term, the increased sales and profits gained in business dealings with rogue states may be tempting. In the long term, they usually exact a high price and destroy more value than they ever created. Ethical failure and corruption both damage value creation. This applies to companies as well as to states. Moral double standards and dependencies trigger crises in companies or sometimes even wars between states. Improving our trading framework isn't protectionism. It is looking after our own interests in a healthy way. In other words, "realpolitik" in its truer, deeper sense. Because the idea of "realpolitik"—politics that privileges the practical over other considerations—also needs a rethink.

No one embodies the concept of realpolitik more than Henry Kissinger. We've known each other for over twenty-five years, and I consider him a friend and one of the towering political intellects of our time. Kissinger systematically established diplomatic relations with both China and Russia during Richard Nixon's and Gerald Ford's eras, with the goal of building close and lasting economic ties. This initially seemed more desirable and rational than confrontational bloc-building between East and West, communism and capitalism. And it was particularly appropriate given the Chinese economic reform and liberalization period that followed under paramount leader Deng Xiaoping. It was the fertile ground in which the idea of "change through trade" grew—for many years to mutual advantage. Kissinger's policy paid off for three decades. But Putin and Xi have changed that. In the long run, it turns out that economic relations not based on genuine, consistent, equal rules give rise to unilateral advantages and unhealthy dependencies. This is what has enabled China's rise as the world's dominant economic power—along with the resurgence of a fractured Soviet Union, thanks to Putin's gas geopolitics.

"Realpolitik" is only deserving of the name when it truly protects our own political and economic interests, when it brings about prosperity, security, peace, and freedom in as many countries around the world as possible—but first and foremost (this much egotism is allowed) in the democracies of the free world. This is "realpolitik" in Kissinger's true and modern sense. This is the realpolitik of the Freedom Trade Alliance.

A new values-based trade policy is the best of all available options.

Europe and the U.S. should form the basis of the Freedom Trade Alliance. But it should include as many nations as possible. Critical mass provides the very best chance of success. America by itself would achieve nothing. It would isolate and weaken itself by decoupling on its own—a large island on the other side of the Atlantic. Europe alone would achieve even less—and become China's Eurasian annex. A transatlantic alliance between the United States and Europe would create a founding axis of free trade, which would quickly attract other free democracies. And for China (1.41 billion inhabitants/GDP of $17.73 trillion) and Russia (143.45 million inhabitants/GDP of $1.78 trillion) the Alliance would become a fact of trading life they can't ignore. If one day Africa (excluding northern regions; 1.18 billion inhabitants/GDP of $1.93 trillion), the Arab world (including the North African countries; 456.52 million inhabitants/GDP of $2.86 trillion), and above all India (1.41 billion inhabitants/GDP of $3.18 trillion) were also to join this alliance of strength, the pull effect would be great enough to cause real behavioral change. Even autocratic superpowers would one day have to rethink the question of whether authoritarian isolationism or pragmatic cooperation is the more suitable basis for sustainable prosperity and stability. Then, at the very latest, a new values-based trade policy would become a magnet for democratization and globalization.

Climate policy will play a crucial role in this process. A trade policy that is also based on binding climate targets must work to ensure that China, the world's largest CO_2 producer—responsible for over a third of all global CO_2 emissions—becomes part of an international strategy. Because this is a more attractive long-term option than separate economic and climate policy paths. Or giving up when it is too late.

Which brings us to the final and perhaps most desperate argument against a new trade strategy: It's already too late. We've passed the point of no return. Our codependency on countries like China has been too great for too long.

This argument is both correct and incorrect. In many respects, it is indeed too late for an immediate, abrupt U-turn. The nature of our current dependencies means that intermediate steps and state support will be needed when implementing a new trade policy. On the other hand, an examination of possible outcomes shows that the negative effects on GDP, while significant, would not be life-threatening for democratic economies. And the stimulus provided by the medium-term effects would far outweigh any risks and losses.

So while it is objectively late in the day it is ultimately not too late. In any case, even if it were too late or almost too late, what alternative do we have? Waiting? For our codependency to turn into a unilateral dependency? For China to decouple from us? For a war over Taiwan? A sudden trade war with China over microchips or antibiotics or AI? Or a conflict with Saudi Arabia over oil and petrodollars? Simply waiting would be much worse than taking very late action. Because action proactively shapes the future, while waiting means simply enduring whatever happens next. The price of passivity is higher. Chaos would cost us more. "Change through trade" didn't work. We must shape "change through action." Freedom must not be traded for business. That's why we need the Freedom Trade Alliance.

During the Renaissance and especially the fifteenth century, Venice was *the* global economic superpower. In the centuries before that, Venice, like all the powers of the time, had based its trade on expansion and conquest. But as other superpowers—such as the Ottoman Empire—grew too strong, a pragmatic reorientation took place. It was Venice that created the earliest, highly successful form of globalization, one that was based on three core principles: truly free trade with its partners, a reliable set of rules (perhaps not exactly "rule of law," but about the closest you could get in those days), and last but not least, welcome to everyone who contributed and complied with the rules—in other words, a modern, tolerant, skill-driven immigration policy.

We may need to re-create some of that Renaissance spirit now.

Only a renaissance of truly free trade can save democracy—and bring about the rebirth of what we once called "liberalism"—

in the non-party-political sense of the word. Liberalism in the spirit of Adam Smith has widely vanished. The "art of the possible" can re-create it.

This is an American-European project. It can only be achieved together. Dedicated to the spirit of the "Liberty Song" by John Dickinson, one of the Founding Fathers of the United States of America: "By uniting we stand, by dividing we fall."

Epilogue: Thirty Minutes with Annalena Baerbock

Annalena Baerbock and I live on the same street, just a few doors apart. But for a long time we've only bumped into each other at political receptions and events in Berlin, and never gotten beyond small talk. At a dinner hosted by the German president in honor of his Israeli counterpart, we chat over drinks and agree to meet for a proper conversation at her office.

On September 26, 2022, I arrive at the Foreign Office just before 6 p.m. The "Haus am Werderschen Markt," as it's known, is only around ten minutes' walk from our Axel Springer offices. The building was constructed as an extension of the Reichsbank—Germany's former central bank—between 1934 and 1940. Here, the Nazis organized the financing of the war, commandeered gold, and distributed reserves from conquered war zones, along with assets expropriated from Jewish families. The National Socialist extermination program was also financed and organized here. From 1959 onward, the building served as the party head-

quarters of the SED, the German Democratic Republic's ruling Socialist Unity Party.

Today, the first female foreign minister in German history has her offices here. She is also the first Green politician to be tasked with implementing—rather than just advocating—a "values-based foreign policy."

There are endless corridors, austere-looking rooms, and wood-paneled walls, with travertine and parquet flooring. The hallway features the German and EU flags, and the G7 conference symbol. After saying her goodbyes to one of her international peers, the federal minister for foreign affairs enters the small meeting room where I'm waiting at a round wooden table with my glass of mineral water.

Annalena Baerbock smiles at me across the table. I ask if she enjoys her job, despite everything. Yes, she replies, even though it's hard to imagine given the terrible situation, but she enjoys what she does. And she is grateful for the opportunity to do it. As she says this, she comes across both a little shy and extremely self-confident.

We talk about a mixture of current issues. First, a brief and relaxed exchange about the not entirely cordial relationship between the Green Party and some Axel Springer publications (the company and the Greens are considered polar opposites by those trading in clichés). Then we discuss the future direction of the Ukraine war and its possible impact on China's behavior. Our analyses are strikingly similar: how Xi and Putin are experimenting with the West; how naïvely many in Germany, in particular, have misinterpreted these autocrats' actions; how for a long time most Americans have held a much more realistic view, especially her counterpart Secretary of State Antony Blinken—in a surprisingly hawkish mindset with regard to Putin's attacks on freedom. We also touch *on the situation in Turkey and the women's uprisings in Iran. And then the conversation takes a more personal turn.*

I ask how she deals with the issue of arms deliveries to Ukraine given that she represents a pacifist party, and what motivated her to enter politics in the first place. I was never a pacifist, but I've always been driven by my belief in international law, Baerbock says. Even early on, that was something that impressed me about the Greens: Their first aim was always a civilian conflict resolution, but in the case of serious human rights violations, they faced up to the dilemma and didn't rule out military intervention. To my surprise, she adds: I actually originally wanted to be a war reporter.

Then Baerbock tells me about her grandfather, who was born in 1913. During World War II, he was a Wehrmacht officer tasked with anti-aircraft gun maintenance. He would tell the young Annalena about the horrors of war and how fortunate her generation was not having to go through all that again. But it was her grandmother who was even more central to her political development. Baerbock tells me all about Alma Choroba, her mother's mother. Even as a child, she admired the strength of the woman who had rolled up her sleeves to help rebuild after the war, and who radiated confidence and joie de vivre despite having experienced so many awful things herself—in wartime, when having to flee, and even afterward. Baerbock recounts an episode that also features in her autobiographical book. Annalenchen, her grandmother said, if the bad men ever come, you must crap yourself—then maybe they'll leave you alone. She only realized later that her grandmother was talking about the trauma of rape. That would certainly explain why her grandmother talked so much to her about the horrors of war during the Bosnian conflict of the 1990s, when mass rapes once again became common in the heart of Europe. She hadn't re-

ally understood all that at the time. But ultimately, her political commitment stems from her grandmother's outlook—a woman so wounded and yet so strong. In the end, it was and still is all about justice.

You can't stay silent in the face of injustice, she says.

One of the main reasons why she went into party politics was the Greens' foreign policy under Joschka Fischer and his stance during the Bosnian War, as well as on Europe. Not just "never again war," but "never again Auschwitz, never again genocide." Her own compass, Baerbock says, has always been guided by human rights and international law. And that helps when dealing with Putin's war. Dictators, says the German foreign minister, understand only one language: showing a clear stance and a show of strength.

Baerbock's secretary interrupts our conversation for a third time. The minister really does need to get on now. On my way down in the elevator, I picture the minister's smile while saying: You can't stay silent in the face of injustice. A new generation is shaping a new kind of politics, both in substance and style. Annalena Baerbock is a green hawk: a leftist "neocon" who views democracy as a universal value and universal right. She has reshaped the concept of German postwar foreign policy more than anybody else— by turning the pacifist founding myth of the Green Party upside down and reversing Angela Merkel's "don't get involved" attitude. The new paradigms are interventionism and NATO solidarity to protect democracy.

I sense a courage that Putin will never understand.

ACKNOWLEDGMENTS

This book was an adventure to which many have contributed. Some are mentioned in the text, others helped with their thoughts, criticism, and editing. I am immensely grateful for all the honest feedback, insights, and energy that have flowed into these lines. Thank you!

INDEX

INDEX

INDEX

INDEX

INDEX

INDEX

Modi, Narendra, 26
Morocco, 109
Muhammad (Prophet), 61
Müller, Herta, 71
Munich Security Conference, 41
Myanmar, 58

National Highway Network Plan, 116
National Interest, The, 15
National Security Legislation Amendment, Australia, 125
National Socialism, 33–34
NATO, 31, 38, 43, 44, 80, 85, 122, 130, 169, 184
Nazism, 33–34
Newcastle United Football Club, 63
Nobel Prizes, 40, 71, 109
Nord Stream 1, 86, 88
Nord Stream 2, 21, 40, 86
North Korea, 50, 60
nuclear power, 39, 86–87, 91

Obama, Barack, 128
Ohlberg, Mareike, 171
Opel, 117
Ostpolitik, 16

Pakistan, 109
Paris agreement, 154
Pelosi, Nancy, 102, 123, 129
Perestroika, 38
Peter the Great, 38
Philippines, 109
photovoltaic industry, 141
Pierer, Heinrich von, 95, 175
PIF (Public Investment Fund), Saudi Arabia, 63

Pillar of Shame (sculpture), 115
PKK (Kurdistan Workers' Party), 71
polarization, political, 80, 82
POLITICO, 130
Poschardt, Ulf, 69
Posta (newspaper), 50
Pratasevich, Raman, 58–59
presidential election, 2020, 82
press freedom, 27, 57–63, 69–77
"Price of Procrastination, The" (Brandenburg Institute for Society and Security), 29
Public Investment Fund (PIF), Saudi Arabia, 63
Putin, Vladimir
 aggression of, 20–21, 25, 182
 and democracy, 37–39
 and Henry Kissinger, 177
 meeting with Döpfner, 7–11
 and Gerhard Schröder, 88
 successors of, 168
 use of alternative facts, 81
 and Yanukovych, 109

Rachman, Gideon, 65–66
"Realpolitik," 176–177
Red Notice (Browder), 67
Ren Zhengfei, 126
Reporters Without Borders, 58
Republic of China (Taiwan), 102, 114–118, 123–125
Roth, Claudia, 74
rule of law, 2, 3, 31, 40, 57, 67, 74, 75, 76, 99, 151–153, 154, 179
Rushdie, Salman, 61–62
Russia, 168–170
 autocracy, 26

INDEX

INDEX

ABOUT THE AUTHOR

Mathias Döpfner is the chairman and CEO of Axel Springer SE, owner of the US media brands *Politico*, *Insider*, and *Morning Brew*, and the largest digital publisher in Europe. He joined the company in 1998 as editor in chief of the German daily *Welt* and became CEO in 2002. Ever since, he has pushed the digital transformation to defend independent quality journalism. He is a member of the board of directors of Netflix and Warner Music Group, serves on the steering committee of the Bilderberg Meeting, and holds an honorary office on the American Jewish Committee. He studied musicology, German literature, and theatrical arts in Boston and Frankfurt, where he also completed his PhD.